Regionalism and the
Reading Class

Regionalism and the Reading Class

WENDY GRISWOLD

The University of Chicago Press ❋ *Chicago and London*

WENDY GRISWOLD
is professor of sociology,
comparative literary
studies, and English at
Northwestern University
and professor II of
sociology at the University
of Oslo, Norway. She is
the author of several books
including *Culture and
Societies in a Changing
World* and *Bearing Witness:
Readers, Writers, and the
Novel in Nigeria.*

The University of Chicago Press, Chicago 60637
The University of Chicago Press, Ltd., London
© 2008 by The University of Chicago
All rights reserved. Published 2008
Printed in the United States of America
16 15 14 13 12 11 10 09 08   1 2 3 4 5
ISBN-13: 978-0-226-30922-4 (cloth)
ISBN-10: 0-226-30922-3 (cloth)

Library of Congress Cataloging-in-Publication Data

Griswold, Wendy.
    Regionalism and the reading class / Wendy Griswold.
        p.   cm.
    Includes bibliographical references and index.
    ISBN-13: 978-0-226-30922-4 (cloth : alk. paper)
    ISBN-10: 0-226-30922-3 (cloth : alk. paper)
    1. Reading—Social aspects.   2. Reading interests.
3. Regionalism—Social aspects.   I. Title.
    LB1050.2 .G75   2008
    418.4—dc22

                                                2007026794

⊗ The paper used in this publication meets the minimum
requirements of the American National Standard for
Information Sciences—Permanence of Paper for Printed
Library Materials, ANSI Z39.48-1992.

Contents

Illustrations

Acknowledgments

My deepest debts are to my coauthors: Fredrik Engelstad (chapter 5), Terrence McDonnell (chapter 2), and Nathan Wright (chapters 2 and 3). I have been blessed to enjoy both their intellectual partnership and their friendship.

Portions of this book have appeared in earlier form. I am grateful to the *American Journal of Sociology*, *Annual Review of Sociology*, *Comparative Social Research*, Elsevier, and *Polis*, for permissions to use these materials. For chapter 3, my thanks go to Valerie May and the National Geographic Society, sponsor of Survey2000, and to James Witte of Clemson University, who was the principle investigator. For chapter 4, thanks go to Mabel Berezin, Gianfranco Poggi, and Marco Santoro and the *Polis* editors.

If all the books that began by thanking University of Chicago Press senior editor Doug Mitchell were put together, they would make up a good-sized library of contemporary sociology. Here is another such book and another thank you. Additional thanks go to Katherine Frentzel, Robert Hunt, and Tim McGovern at the Press; it has been a pleasure working with them.

Gail Reinertsen is exemplary as a regionalist, as a cowbird, as a reading class stalwart, and as a sister. I dedicate *Regionalism and the Reading Class* to her with love and admiration.

Introduction: Regionalism and the Reading Class

This book makes two claims. First, cultural regionalism, and regional literature in particular, is flourishing. Moreover, it is flourishing not despite globalization and information technologies, but because of them. Second, a reading class, habitual readers of print with a distinct demographic profile, has emerged from the general public. This reading class is modest in size but intense in its literary practices and in its cultural influence. Both of these claims contradict the conventional wisdom about contemporary culture.

People have voiced concerns about global cultural homogeneity obliterating people's "sense of place" since the colonial-era condemnation of cultural imperialism. Globalization, state centralization of cultural power, international consumerism, "McDonaldization," and the triumphant march of information technology have only exacerbated the fears. Nevertheless, a considerable amount of research is showing that people refashion external cultural inputs to conform to local sensibilities. Specifically, people use the very elements of globalized, electronic culture to rediscover, invent, fashion, promote, and celebrate their place-specific distinctiveness. Regional culture is part of this process, and this book demonstrates that literary regionalism has benefited from the developments that some had thought would kill it off.

A great deal has been said about the decline of leisure reading and about how print is losing the competition with other forms of entertainment, particularly electronic media. Reading is "at risk," according to one prominent study, and the decline of reading is a serious public problem. Nevertheless, this book suggests that such a view could benefit from a historical perspective. Readers in most societies have almost always been a minority. Only in a small portion of the world (northwest Europe, North America, and—somewhat later—Japan) and only for a brief period of time (mid-nineteenth to mid-twentieth century) was reading the standard pastime for the middle-class majority. The more typical situation is the one that is increasingly the case today: readers are an elite group that holds disproportionate political, economic, and cultural power. To recognize this as a fact is neither to decry the elitism nor to celebrate the avidity of committed readers, but it is to gain a clearer sense of where the practice of reading stands now and in the foreseeable future.

While the two claims—about regionalism and about the reading class—can each stand alone, the book makes a third claim: that the first two are connected. The reading class is an active agent that is constantly reinforcing regionalism. Paradoxically, educated, mobile people, frequent flyers, elites who command technological, economic, and political advantages, work hard at putting down cultural roots. Under the right conditions, members of this group can be cultural cowbirds who demonstrate their cosmopolitanism through an intense localism.

This book shows when and how the reading class produces regionalism.

Place, Regional Culture, and Regional Literature

People make places so they can know where they are. A popular movie convention expresses this: regaining consciousness after being knocked out, the first thing the detective or cowboy mumbles is, "Where am I?"

Where am I? This urge for location is both a biological drive and a collective necessity. Some answers to "Where am I?" are factually right but socially wrong. The response cannot be "You're in Asia" or "In a narrow bed" or "At x degrees latitude and y degrees longitude," although these may indeed be true. Appropriate answers are either institutional ("You're in the hospital, Marco") or else refer to a mapped and named landscape ("We're still in Shanghai, Melissa"). An explanatory statement usually follows: "You're in the hospital, Marco; you've been in an accident." "We're still in Shanghai, Melissa; the kidnappers have locked us in this warehouse." These socially correct answers satisfy the questioner by establishing location according to a shared system of place classification. The person is not just "coming to" consciousness, but coming to place.

This chapter considers what exactly a place is and how people make one. It focuses on cultural expressions of place, both in the more passive form of regional culture and in the more assertive form of regionalism. It then turns to literature and the aesthetic structure of literary regionalism, rooted in classical pastoral and encountered most often in the contemporary regional mystery. Examples of these genres will flesh out the understanding of how regional literature operates and why its appeal is so strong.

Place

Understanding one's place within a system of places orients people not just geographically, but also socially. Such orientation is vital for both individual identity and interpersonal communication. Meeting someone for the first time, we ask, "Where are you from?" Although the reply is typically irrelevant in that almost nobody relates to a new acquaintance differently because she comes from Toronto rather than from Vancouver, nevertheless the information eases the way to further conversation based on some common understanding of "Toronto." This is possible because we share a rough-and-ready regionalism that allows us to infer certain things about people based upon the scanty data of where they "are from." We "place" people, at least provisionally, by drawing on this shared knowledge.

Place is less a geographic fact than a human accomplishment. It is both socially produced and socially productive. A great deal of energy goes into the demarcation of place, the separation of the "figure" of a certain place from the "ground" of all the places it abuts; this is the social production of place. Conversely, places can influence behavior, thought, and feeling; this is their productive capacity. Although place may be experienced on the level of the individual, as when someone fondly remembers the place where he first fell in love, more often it is collective and shared. Everyone in a small town, for example, knows where the teenagers go parking, while newcomers to cities are warned about which neighborhoods are considered unsafe. Usually this is just local knowledge, people being at home in a certain place, knowing the boundaries, the spatial symbols, "the way we do things around here." It is exceptional when the characteristics and quirks of a place become known beyond the place itself.

Place stands in contrast to space. Space is an empty theatre in which something may or may not happen. When something does happen, we say it "takes place," and the space becomes a place. Places where nothing much happens, nothing significant to people at any rate, tend to revert to spaces: abandoned urban neighborhoods, the desert, wide open spaces, outer space. Even places filled with human activity can be perceived as voids if the activities are meaningless in themselves and the people just passing through; at airports the long corridors leading to the gates have this empty quality—more space than place—no matter how crowded they are.[1]

Yi-Fu Tuan, an influential theorist of human geography, argues that whereas space is an object of thought, place is "a center of meaning constructed by experience." People experience place at different levels:

> To know a place fully means both to understand it in an abstract way and to know it as one person knows another. At a high theoretical level, places are points in a spatial system. At the opposite extreme, they are strong visceral feelings. Places are seldom known at either extreme: the one is too remote from sensory experience to be real,

---

1. Pico Iyer (2000) has celebrated such non-places as airports as being the natural settings for the "global soul," the cosmopolitan who has multiple homes and no home. "This creature could be a person who had grown up in many cultures at once—and so lived in the cracks between them—or might be one who, though rooted in background, lived and worked on a globe that propelled him from tropic to snowstorm in three hours. She might have a name that gave away nothing about her nationality (a name like Kim, say, or Maya, or Tara), and she might have a porous sense of self that changed with her location . . . The Global Soul, to use the convenient tag, lived in the metaphorical equivalent of international airspace" (18–19). Although Iyer overplays his hand, as when he remarks that the question "Were do you come from?" is "coming to seem as antiquated an inquiry as 'What regiment do you belong to?,'" his meditations on airports and other non-places are arresting. In a series of books on such non-place places as gas stations, motels, and fast food restaurants, John Jakle and Keith Sculle have shown how standardization, what they call the combination of place-product-packaging, celebrates the "nowhere" qualities of its own creation (Jakle and Sculle 1994, 1999, 2004; Jakle, Sculle, and Rogers 1996).

and the other presupposes rootedness in a locality and an emotional commitment to it that are increasingly rare. To most people in the modern world, places lie somewhere in the middle range of experience.

Places are not static, however, and cultural work can move a place closer to one extreme or another. Such movement, as activated through literature, will be a central theme of this book.[2]

Space weighed heavily on pre-modern peoples. Most of the world was unknown and avoided, while the familiar areas were named and put to use, i.e., converted into places. Often some spirit, a genius loci, was in charge of a particular place and required sacrifices. People divided the known landscape between productive and sacred places. What people could do in a particular place—whether they could farm in it, hunt in it, or bury their dead in it—depended on its physical features and spiritual status.[3]

Today the unknown areas of the planet have all but disappeared. People impose themselves on space, instead of being subject to it. Rationalization turned space into something to be mastered, explored, and mapped. The European "discovery" of the "New World" was both fundamental to and representative of this development. Modern men and women feel a horror from unmapped space, "the heart of darkness."

Not only have places been named and mapped, but the physical characteristics of place have diminished impact on most people. Three-quarters or more of the population in industrialized countries now live in cities, and poorer countries are rapidly urbanizing as well. Accompanying these changes has been a rev-

2. Tuan, Yi-Fu (1975, 152). I am generally adhering to Tuan's definition in this book, reserving "space" for more impersonal, abstract units and divisions, "place" for meaningful ones. Not every author follows this usage, however, and I will use the terminology of the authors themselves, e.g., when Cole (2004) talks about "sacred spaces."

3. For an elaboration of the division between productive and sacred spaces and how rituals managed the sacred spaces to secure benefits for the ancient Greeks, see Cole (2004).

olution in speed of communications and transportation, which has changed the way people view the world. Few places seem distant when you can fly to them in a matter of hours; few people seem far away when you can keep in touch by mobile phone or e-mail. Technology has leaped previously impassable spatial barriers, not once but repeatedly, with each new development able to carry more complex forms of communication. English has become the first true world language, with airlines and teenagers leading the way. In such a world, isolation has become a social problem but not a spatial one.[4]

Paradoxically, as space itself became less important, industrialization brought about finer distinctions among places. Modern production entailed a sharp separation between private (domestic) and public (work, political life) places, the home and the workplace. This change had an early phase, the congregation of workers in urban neighborhoods developing around factories and commercial sites, and a later one, the development of suburbs whereby people could—and chose to—live at some distance from their place of employment. The separation of dwelling and employment gave rise to what Ray Oldenburg has called "third places," accessible neighborhood joints like taverns or beauty salons, neither work nor home, that fostered sociability and community.[5]

---

4. According to the Population Reference Bureau (2005), "The world has experienced unprecedented urban growth in recent decades. In 2000, about 47 percent of the world's population lived in urban areas, about 2.8 billion. There are 411 cities over 1 million. More developed nations are about 76 percent urban, while 40 percent of residents of less developed countries live in urban areas. However, urbanization is occurring rapidly in many less developed countries. It is expected that 60 percent of the world population will be urban by 2030, and that most urban growth will occur in less developed countries." For the time/space revolution of modernity, see Kern (1983); for the pathologies of social isolation in spite of spatial proximity, see Klinenberg (2002).

5. Oldenburg (1989). During the past few years sociologists have given renewed attention to "place" as a variable (Gieryn 2000). To take one prominent example, inner city neighborhoods are being seen as cultural worlds, not simply as economic and structural products. Douglas Massey and Nancy Denton (1994) studied the devastating impact that inner-city spatial isolation—"American apartheid"—has on African Americans. Ethnographers probe the symbolic and aesthetic worlds such conditions produce,

Modernity made explicit spatial distinctions at the global level as well. Pre-modern political formations included large, shifting empires, small societies with sacred centers but uncertain frontiers, and vast areas controlled by whatever warlord was currently on the scene. The modern era, in contrast, is one of nation-states. Specific countries had specific colonies under nineteenth-century colonialism, as when the Conference of Berlin (1884–85) divided Africa among the European powers. Wars end with treaties that specify maps, lines where one country ends and another begins. Passports, immigration controls, and national coins, flags, stamps, airlines—all are emblematic of the modern age. Countries may be imaginary, as Benedict Anderson has famously suggested, but these imagined communities have had a hard-and-fast quality that has heretofore seemed inescapable.[6]

Although both control of space and a precise, rational division among places have been the hallmarks of the industrial era, post-modernity seems to bring changes in how people encounter spatiality. Multiple dimensions of globalization—constant flows of people, of goods, of ideas, of money, of images, of information—accelerated by the information-technology revolution have made conceivable a world in which space has become so utterly mastered as to be utterly unimportant. The very spatial divisions of modernity, such as those between countries or between work and home, have started to break down.

Yet oddly enough, though spatial boundaries may be evaporating, space—even in the abstract—seems to be gaining new importance. People manipulate it through everything from feng shui to New Urbanism. Time and space seem bound up in one another rather than being separate dimensions of experience. A

---

as when Elijah Anderson analyzes the intricate set of signs and behaviors that black youth must master to steer between trouble with the police and with their peers (E. Anderson 1999; cf. Suttles 1972). Mitchell Duneier (1999) studies the sidewalk, where the worlds of the very poor and the middle class intersect. While this type of local knowledge is often at the level of neighborhood, the deployment of signifiers to assert identities and to mark and defend territory may operate at any level.

6. Anderson (1983/1991). See Torpey (2000) for a political history of passports; see Wagner-Pacifici (2005) for the ritualization of treaties ending wars.

chat room (space) is defined by time, i.e., by who is online at the moment. "Face time" is the increasingly rare coming together of people in a single space. Environmentalism has promoted conceiving of space as a socially shaped object; a wilderness is only "empty space" according to one human definition of "what counts" (e.g., productivity) vs. another (e.g., nature). And not everyone gets to define what counts; postmodern geographers are acutely aware of the gendered and power dimensions of spatial organization.[7]

The urge for location, the need for emplacement, has not diminished with the changing configuration of the spatial. If place is "a center of meaning constructed by experience," then people need place because they need meaning. Space becomes place by accruing meaning. Place is particularistic, emotion-laden, bound up with memory.

Turning space into place involves mapping, and while mapping can be done by cartographers and surveyors, it can also be done by words. This is what folklorist Kent Ryden has called "mapping the invisible landscape." He contends that the landscape is space, without significance, until history and memory

7. Similarly, temporal boundaries are less significant, as in the global financial markets operating on a twenty-four-hour basis, yet postmodern men and women are obsessed with time, its quality, its extension. Karl Marx (1993, 539) wrote that under the industrial capitalism characteristic of the modern epoch, "capital must on the one side strive to tear down every spatial barrier to intercourse, i.e., to exchange, and conquer the whole earth for its market, it strives on the other side to annihilate this space [of circulation] with time, i.e., to reduce to a minimum the time spent in motion from one place to another. The more developed the capital, therefore, the more extensive the market over which it circulates, which forms the spatial orbit of its circulation, the more does it strive simultaneously for an even greater extension of the market and for the greater annihilation of space by time." But if time eclipsed space, now that which is historically separate can be brought together, as in postmodern architecture or Disney-esque juxtapositions. Former sites of production become zones of consumption, as when factories become lofts in gentrifying neighborhoods (Zukin 1982, 1991). Free trade zones and global cities operate outside of the rules of the nation-state, and their development is on a different trajectory from the rest of the nation (Sassen 2001). Such changes lead to the suspicion that certain spaces are cut loose from history. For discussions of the relationship between power and space, see the excellent collection *NowHere* put together by Friedland and Boden (1994).

have written meanings upon it, whereupon it becomes a place. While the meaningless quality of uncharted space is the most obvious invisible landscape, Ryden focuses on places whose meaning has eroded. Such erosion can happen through physical changes, through the sheer passage of time, and through the loss of people who remember. Words can recover such a landscape and restore it to visibility.

In Louisiana, for example, the logging industry decimated the cypress swamps by clear-cutting in the early twentieth-century. Eventually the first-growth cypress were all but gone, the sawmills closed, and the memory of the logging boom years faded. Following Ryden's analysis, if such a landscape were to return to or retain visibility, it would be via words. Songs about the loggers, a roadside plaque marking where the mill once stood, or a cautionary tale about environmental destruction are verbal forms of landscape restoration. So is a formal work of literature such as Tim Gautreaux's prize-winning novel *The Clearing*, which drew attention to the Louisiana loggers in the 1920s and their social and natural landscape.[8]

Places become lost and found; landscapes move in and out of visibility. This can be a physical process—Pompeii thriving, buried, forgotten, remembered, excavated, restored—or it can be a verbal one, through media, like stories, folklore, or memories passed down through families. A woman points to a chimney poking out of an empty field and tells her granddaughter, "That was where the old Kellogg place was, before the fire. What a sad family that was. You see, Geoffrey Kellogg was a drinker, and one night..." And the field becomes a place, visible, mapped.

8. Gautreaux, considered one of the most important contemporary regionalists, lives and writes about southeastern Louisiana. Gautreaux's stories have appeared in such highly visible publications as *Harper's, Atlantic Monthly,* and *Prize Stories: The O. Henry Awards.* His first novel, *The Next Step in the Dance* (1998), won the 1999 Southeastern Book Sellers Association Award, and his second, *The Clearing* (2003), won the 2003 Mid-South Independent Booksellers Association Award. A National Endowment for the Arts Fellow, Gautreaux is currently writer-in-residence at Southeastern Louisiana University, from which he retired after over three decades of teaching. For the "invisible landscape," see Ryden (1993).

At least for a time, for words may fail, and places, unmoored from their stories, may revert to emptiness, mere space.[9]

Such verbal mapping provides orientation, confirms identity, and creates meaningfulness. Emily Dickinson described this verbal place-making in her poem about a prairie:

> To make a prairie it takes a clover and one bee,
> One clover, and a bee,
> And revery.
> The revery alone will do,
> If bees are few.

Only revery—thoughts organized into words, like a poem—are needed to map the landscape and make its open spaces into a place, the prairie.

A prairie is an ecological system involving tall grasses. But if we use the definite article, *the* prairie is a region. When Americans refer to "the prairie," they do not mean just any grassland but the ones in the upper Midwest—Illinois, Iowa, Minnesota, part of the Dakotas, and up into Canada. What magic makes some grasslands "the prairie," even once the grasses have mostly been paved over, while another grassland is just any old prairie? This is where regions and regionalism come into the picture.

Regional culture[10]

Regionalism, at its most basic, is a recognized association between culture and place. "You're from Toronto? Great city— I hear it's very cosmopolitan. Lots of good places to eat? Supposed to be quite a music scene there. And culture—Margaret Atwood is one of my favorite writers. What about the winters?"

---

9. Ryden (1993); cf. Lowenthal (1985). Abandoned houses are especially evocative in this place-to-space movement; see Raban (1996) or the Edwin Arlington Robinson poem entitled "The House on the Hill."

10. An early version of this section appeared in the 2001 edition of the *International Encyclopedia of the Social and Behavior Sciences* under the heading of "Regionalism and Cultural Expression" (Griswold 2001b).

Crude, stereotypical, widely shared regionalism makes such chatter meaningful. People use cognitive schemas to categorize one another—gender, ethnicity, religion, nationality, age, class, sexual orientation—and region is one of the these primary classifiers. Although asking "Where are you from?" is more socially acceptable than "What's your sexual orientation?" the goal is the same: to elicit categorical information so as to make some rough guesses about what the other person is like. All of these categories make sense only in terms of a system of categories. "Toronto" means little by itself: a place has meaning largely with reference to a system of places (e.g., Toronto versus Montreal; Ontario versus British Columbia; the Canadian Shield versus the Maritimes versus the Interior Plains; Canada versus the U.S.; etc.).[11]

The term "region" usually designates a patch of geography, the borders of which do not correspond to the borders of an individual country. Regions can be entirely within countries, e.g., Provence; they can include several countries, e.g., Scandinavia; they can cut across countries, e.g., the North American prairie, the Sahel. Sometimes regions are congruent with political boundaries—Tuscany is one of twenty Italian *regioni*—but more often regional boundaries are fuzzy, one region shading off into another, and depend on the viewer's perspective.

Regions do not simply fit together like pieces of a puzzle, although people often envision them that way for administrative or analytic reasons. Any point on the globe can be seen as part of any number of nested or overlapping regions. If a Florentine poet were to appear in a "regional" anthology, for example, the "region" could be Tuscany, central Italy, southern Europe, or the Mediterranean. Region is less a geographic fact than a social convention. Nevertheless, most people think of a region as a more-or-less fixed geographic zone—the Arctic, the Great Plains, West Africa, Polynesia—even if its boundaries are arguable. Typically the geographic region has political and economic

---

11. For sociological considerations of the role of schemas in cognition, see DiMaggio (1997), Zerubavel (1997), and Wuthnow (2006).

implications (the Canadian Maritimes) and/or ethnic ones (the Kurdish region). Although ethnic regions are not always geographically contiguous, the term is not used if there is no geographic specificity whatsoever; no one refers to "the Gypsy region."

The people within a region are seen as having something in common. This common ground, which is typically geographic, political, and/or economic, gives rise to shared forms of cultural expression. The inverse is true as well; shared cultural features may encourage political or economic linkage. *Regional culture* refers to cultural objects—arts, crafts, ways of speaking, cooking styles, modes of dress, architecture—that bear a socially recognized relationship to some place, usually their place of origin. Such a relationship may take place on any level, from the local to the transnational. Regional culture expresses place. It also creates it.

Even when regions are demarcated strictly by geography, some degree of common culture emerges. Climate, topography, and relationships to the sea will influence agricultural and commercial activities, and these in turn give rise to some cultural commonalities, regardless of differences in other dimensions. Cuisine is an example: political antagonists like the Palestinians and Israelis prepare similar food in similar ways. Absent such obvious conflict, some overlap between geography and culture is simply taken for granted. Geographers can divide Canadian aboriginal tribes into six geographic categories such as Arctic and Northwest Coast, as figure 1 shows, thereby implying that each of the six shares some cultural common ground. Such regionalism seems natural, the straightforward products of material circumstances and history. These shared characteristics constitute what we might call the weak version of regional culture.

Regional culture also comes in a strong version, more assertive and self-aware. Geographer D. W. Meinig defined this type of regional culture as "that which is characteristic of a group of people who are deep-rooted and dominant in a particular territory, who are conscious of their identity as deriving from a common heritage, and who share a common language and basic patterns

FIGURE I. Aboriginal cultural areas of Canada

of life." This more self-conscious, more emotionally charged version of regional culture can be distinguished by the term *regionalism*. Regionalism aggressively promotes its own cultural expression. Regionalism in art, for example, is a sharply distinctive and celebratory depiction of the culture of place, as in the Midwestern regionalist painters (notably Grant Wood, Thomas Hart Benton, and John Steuart Curry) of the 1930s. Regionalism is not ignorance of the world beyond—when people think *their* world is *the* world, they are provincials, not regionalists—but the assertion of distinctiveness in relation to that outside world.[12]

Some sociologists in the 1930s, whose research can be seen as the scholarly parallel to the regionalist movement in art, studied regional distinctiveness and its costs and benefits. The best known of these was the team Howard W. Odum assembled at

12. Meinig (1986, 80). For the American regionalist artists, see Dennis (1998).

the University of North Carolina at Chapel Hill. This group produced a series of studies suggesting that the South remained backward because it lacked social institutions that could facilitate social change while protecting traditional culture. The result was that Old South die-hards were stuck in the past, the pro-business New South was unable to reconcile change with continuity, and the result was a divided and stagnant sectionalism. Odum and colleagues argued that the South needed to transform its debilitating local culture by blending it with national aspirations to produce a true regionalism, in which (in his somewhat idiosyncratic definition) the local was integral to the larger unity. They saw literary and cultural regionalism as an undeniable fact—they catalogued over two thousand regionalist titles from two decades of *Publishers Weekly*—but rather than dismissing this as local-color provincialism, Odum and his team maintained that "regional portraitures are only fundamental units in the great American literary fabric." Regionalism, in other words, supported both region and nation.[13]

Although there has been sporadic scholarly interest in regionalism since then, in recent years many people have questioned whether regional cultures, in either weak or strong versions, will survive the homogenization that seems inherent to advanced industrial capitalism and an interconnected world. Place seems to matter less than it used to. Fewer people are rooted in the land. Geography—climate, waterways, soil, topography, natural resources—no longer has a constant and obvious impact on most

13. Odum and Moore (1938); the quotation beginning "regional portraitures" is from p. 43. Odum regarded sectionalism as a pathological form of localism, the result of cultural inbreeding, although many contended that this regional/sectional distinction was hard to maintain. In a similar vein, contemporary political scientist Robert Putnam (1993) has made the case that some regional cultures are healthy for the nation as a whole because they are conducive to democratic politics and political participation. Using data from Italy's twenty administrative regions, Putnam shows how "institutional performance"—effectiveness of and satisfaction with regional government—is high in Italy's north and low in the south, a difference he attributes to different civic traditions in the regional cultures.

people's lives. The economic activities, consumption patterns, recreation, and personal comfort of someone living in Anchorage do not differ greatly from those of her counterpart in Houston. In the world of electronic communications and unrestricted cultural flows, place-based configurations like "region" and "regional culture" have seemed increasingly irrelevant, being little more than constructed authenticity, productions for a tourist market intent on collecting scenic memorabilia.[14]

The "no sense of place" thesis, which Joshua Meyrowitz has argued with great force and which many others have simply assumed, maintains that electronic media has severed the link between social place and physical place. "[A]s place and information access become disconnected, place-specific behaviors and activities begin to fade." Globalization and ICTs (information and communications technologies) are bleaching local color out of the postmodern fabric. This view that local cultures are everywhere endangered is confirmed by resistance, specifically popular expression in resistance to McDonalds in France and Wal-Marts in small towns, in movements like Slow Foods and consumer advocates of "buying local," and in curriculum battles where parents demand "local control" of the schools.[15]

Yet other scholars, impressed by the persistence and assertiveness of place-based social formations, question this inevitable decline of regional and local distinctiveness. From urban turfs to ancestral homelands, place continues to be something people cherish and, indeed, are willing to die for. As people have greater choices about where to live and work, place characteristics themselves have become a key attraction, a point Richard Florida has stressed with respect to members of the "creative class." Proliferation of communications channels encourages formation of new possibilities for the assertion and communication of cultural

14. The steady trickle of scholarship on American regionalism includes Fischer (1989), Gastil (1975), Griffin and Doyle (1995), Jensen (1952), Jordan (1994), and Reed (1986).

15. The "no sense of place" thesis is that of Joshua Meyrowitz (1985); the quotation is from p. 148. Dean MacCannell (1976) set out the postmodern theory of tourism.

identities, and in some cases regionalism seems to find new life through these media.[16]

This leads to the hypothesis that the regionalist impulse is not likely to atrophy, regardless of changes in mobility or communications technology. Making space into place, "mapping the invisible landscape" through words and symbols, is a cultural process that, while by no means innocent of politics and economics, fulfills a human need for meaningful spatial orientation. Regionalism and the culture of place represent, following this line of thought, a psychologically fundamental form of cultural expression. If people define regional cultures as real, they are real in their consequences.[17]

Impulse is not enough, however. For any place-based culture to persist, whether in traditional or newly crafted forms, there has to be people who know it, produce it, respond to it, and pass it along. Regional cooking, for instance, would disappear if no one enjoyed it, if no one prepared it in their kitchens, sought it out in restaurants, or wrote columns and books about it. Such activities transform a local set of practices into an internally valued and externally recognized cultural object. A prime example of regional culture that can be produced, received, honored, and supported by institutions both within and beyond the region itself is regional literature.

Literary Regionalism

What makes literature regional? This question has three answers. The first is aesthetic: certain literary works have content that

16. Logan and Molotch (1987), for example, show how place becomes a selling point for development in the "urban growth machine"; Florida (2002) discusses which kinds of places draw "the creative class." Scholars have recently addressed the lines along which regionalism gets configured (Ayers et al. 1996), the circumstances under which regionalism expands (Griswold and Engelstad 1998), the ability of regional culture to offer a viable alternative to class and racial hierarchies (Stack 1996; Falk 2004), and the degree to which regionalism influences social and political behavior (Putnam 1993).

17. Early twentieth-century sociologist W. I. Thomas famously noted, "If men define situations as real, they are real in their consequences."

mark them as regional. The second is intentional: certain writers intend their works to cluster together in a regional school or movement. The third is institutional: readers, booksellers, publishers, teachers, and reviewers label or frame certain writers and, to a lesser extent, certain literary works as being "regional," regardless of the works' contents or the authors' intentions. These three can overlap in practice but are analytically distinct. This chapter concentrates on the first of these, the regionalist aesthetic, which is the one most intrinsic to the cultural object and least dependent on human interpretation. The case studies of chapters 4–7 will concentrate on the second two processes, regionalist movements and regional framing.

A look at the relationship between food and place helps clarify the regionalist aesthetic. Regional cuisines emphasize local ingredients first and foremost: locally grown fruits and vegetables, wild game and seafood, native grains, and livestock raised on area farms. They emphasize cooking styles that rely on locally available foodstuffs—frying with olive oil in Greece, with butter in Denmark, with palm oil in Nigeria—and locally mastered techniques, such as reconstituting "saltfish" (dried cod) in the West Indies. They feature festival and holiday feasts (e.g., Thanksgiving) that create an emotional and cognitive association between the local culture's seasonal rhythms and its foodstuffs.

On the other hand, some regional foods are made from ingredients available anywhere. In this respect they resemble literature, for words are available anywhere. How do such foods become regionally identified? Here we see both intention and institutional processes at work. Soft drinks are a common example. Moxie is a soda pop from Maine and mostly drunk there; Cheerwine is from North Carolina. Neither contains anything native to its particular state. Moxie and Cheerwine depend not on local ingredients but on a local taste for the product, aided and abetted by marketing and by nostalgia.[18]

18. Cheerwine contains "Carbonated water, sugar and/or corn sweetener, caramel color, phosphoric acid, sodium benzoate (preservative), caffeine, citric acid, natural

FIGURE 2. Cheerwine ad from the 1950s

FIGURE 3. Cheerwine country

Some food is regional through its actual content (local ingredients and techniques), some through its creator's intentions (an upscale restaurant may assert regionalism through its decor and some signature dishes, even though the chef uses considerable non-local ingredients and non-traditional techniques), and some through institutional processes (a recipe or restaurant gets framed as "regional" by food columnists or by marketing). The same three routes to regionalism apply to other cultural objects: art, architecture, design, and of course literature.

Content is particularly interesting. Regional culture does not always have local ingredients, but it does tend toward certain patterns and qualities that add up to a general aesthetic of regionalism. Common characteristics of this aesthetic include the use of local ingredients, reference to local climate and natural resources, simplicity of design, and selective representation of the past through history, tradition, or nostalgia. While none of these is a sine qua non for a regionalist cultural object, at least one must be present. Maine's regional foods, for example, include lobster (local ingredients), baked beans (simplicity; tradition), and Moxie (nostalgia).

What, then, is regional literature? Once again we look to content or aesthetic attributes, to intentionality, and to institutional framing. In the broadest sense, regional literature can be anything written by someone from or associated with a region. Continuing the Maine example, Edna St. Vincent Millay was born in the state and attended high school there, but she left when she went to Vassar College. Later she lived the bohemian life of Greenwich Village in the 1920s, traveled the world, and settled in upstate New York. Most of her poetry was placeless, sonnets and lyrics about love and emotions. Nevertheless institutions have firmly placed her in the pantheon of Maine authors: bookstores and libraries in the state shelve her with the "Maine

---

and artificial flavors, FD&C #40." The list for Moxie is virtually identical, with the addition of something called "gentian root extractives." As a part-time Mainer, I've known about Moxie for a long time, and I'm grateful to Gary Alan Fine, a part-time North Carolinian, for introducing me to Cheerwine.

writers," the state honors her as one of its notables, she is taught in courses on Maine writers, and a statue of her holding her first book gazes over Camden harbor. Millay's sonnets are the literary equivalent of Cheerwine: locally revered even though their ingredients could have come from anywhere.[19]

Regional literature, like regional culture more generally, comes in a strong version as well, one derived from aesthetic content and structure, not just framing. While different regions provide different materials, regionalist writing from anywhere presents some common characteristics. The works that are most readily recognized as "regionalism" share features that amount to a family resemblance. The most important literary expressions of the regional aesthetic are:

- Rural or small-town settings
- Working-class or rustic characters, depicted as tough, unyielding, traditional
- Closely observed descriptions of land, weather, flora, fauna, folkways
- Plots driven by conflict between insiders and outsiders; outsiders (often urban) are agents of change who threaten local way of life
- Reference to the past, to simpler ways now disappearing
- Tension over insider/outsider differences in reading, writing, education, intellectual sophistication

The last takes two forms: one in which locals express a deep suspicion of reading, writing, and/or education, and the other, its opposite, in which the locals, who have been dismissed by the outsiders as rubes, display their learning or cleverness. These six, the markers of the regionalist literary aesthetic, are almost always present in regional novels.

Naturally, even those writers who satisfy the regionalist aesthetic criteria in some of their work do not invariably write in the regional mode. Norwegian Nobel laureate Knut Hamsun, for example, wrote *The Growth of the Soil*, a regionalist classic depicting hardscrabble life in the interior northern Norway. Its protagonist

19. Unlike her sonnets, some of Millay's early poetry, especially the title poem of her first collection, *Renascence*, did have some Maine content.

wrests a farm out of the wilderness; its drama involves unsettling visitors and fateful trips the farmer or his wife make outside the region; it is rich with description of rural people's struggles with the elements and with each other. On the other hand, Hamsun's best-known novel is *Hunger*, which portrays an alienated intellectual starving himself in Kristiana (Oslo) and which could take place in any large city. Hamsun is generally regarded more as a modernist than a regionalist.[20]

To understand how the regionalist aesthetic works, we will first look at a literary masterpiece: *The Day of the Owl (Il Giorno della Civetta)*. Leonardo Sciascia's novel, published in 1961, tells of the murder of a Sicilian contractor who had refused to pay protection to the Mafia, and the subsequent investigation by the Carabinieri. The plot centers on Captain Bellodi, who investigates the murder, eventually figures out what happened, but is stymied by silence and corruption at every level. The regionalist aesthetic unfolds as follows:[21]

(1) Rural or small town settings. In the opening scene a killer shoots Colasberna as he runs to catch a bus for Palermo. This takes place in the town of S., a "poverty-stricken place"; the reader knows it to be a small town because the missing man, Nicolosi, is said to come from B., "another village." Bellodi commands the Carabinieri Company in C., a larger town.

(2) Working-class or rustic characters, depicted as tough, unyielding, traditional. Colasberna's brothers feel shame while they wait to be questioned by the Carabinieri, and they reflect that "Compared to shame, death is nothing." Other locals include a tree pruner and his wife, various construction workers, and peasants. At one point the sergeant-major remarks that Sicilians

20. Hamsun (1859–1952) spent most of his youth in Hamarøy, Nordland, roughly 100 miles north of the Arctic Circle. After much traveling and living various places, including in Chicago, North Dakota, and Minneapolis in the United States, in Finland, in Copenhagen, and in Oslo, Hamsun returned to a Nordland farm in 1911. He published *Markens Grøde* (*The Growth of the Soil*), which was set in this region, in 1917.

21. *Il Giorno della Civetta* was first published in 1961 by Adelphi Edizioni. It was translated into English in 1963; the quotations come from the 2003 *New York Review of Books* edition.

will never tell the authorities anything: "'It's like squeezing tripe: nothing comes out,' he said, meaning the Colasberna brothers, their partners, the town in general and Sicily as a whole" (22). Fear of the Mafia encourages silence. After the shooting, the bus passengers avoid being questioned by the Carabinieri: "With seeming nonchalance, looking around as if they were trying to gauge the proper distance from which to admire the belfry, they drifted off to the sides of the square and, after a last look around, scuttled into alley-ways" (10). Similarly when the sergeant-major questions an eye witness who was standing next to the man who fired the shots, he gets a maddening response: "'Why,' asked the fritter-seller, astonished and inquisitive, 'has there been a shooting?'" (13).

(3) Closely observed descriptions of land, weather, flora, fauna, folkways. Sciascia sketches the essence of the place through both social and natural description: "Sicily is all a realm of fantasy and what can anyone do there without imagination" (35). The missing Nicolosi "must have been invited to some farmhouse party, you know, a fat lamb and lots of wine, then he probably went to sleep it off in a haystack . . ."(22). The *chiarchiaro* is a stony wasteland, "incongruous in green uplands, looked like a huge, black-holed sponge soaking up the light flooding the landscape" (85), and when Nicolosi's body is found there, "The captain thought: 'This is where god throws in the sponge,' associating the sight of the *chiarchiaro* with the struggle and defeat of God in the human heart" (85). Meanwhile the sergeant, a local, appeals to the captain's fondness for Sicilian folk culture ("he knew the captain was interested in popular sayings") by reciting a dialect poem about an owl telling its young they would all meet in the *chiarchiaro*, meaning in death.

(4) Plots driven by conflict between insiders and outsiders; outsiders (often urban) agents of change who threaten local way of life. Captain Bellodi is "an Emilian from Parma" (30). When he enters the station, the Colasberna brothers "thought, with a mixture of relief and scorn, 'A mainlander.' Mainlanders are decent enough, but just don't understand things" (16). A local

Mafioso remarks "Let's hope our Honourable Member gets him [Bellodi] sent back north to eat polenta" (25). When interviewing Nicolosi's widow, "The captain began to talk about Sicily, at its loveliest when most rugged and barren; and how intelligent the Sicilians were. An archaeologist had told him how swift and deft the peasants were during excavations, much more than specialized workmen from the North. It's not true, he said, that Sicilians are lazy or lack initiative." Then he goes on "passing Sicilian literature in review from Verga to *The Leopard*... The woman understood little of this..." (42). Thus does a northern polenta-eater endeavor to instruct a Sicilian about her local culture.

(5) Reference to the past, to simpler ways now disappearing. While Sciascia represents the peasantry with considerable affection, the Sicilian past is more problematic than that of many regional novels because the past represents ignorance and cowering before the Mafia. Many characters refer with some nostalgia to when Mori was in control; Cesare Mori was Mussolini's Prefect of Palermo who launched an aggressive anti-Mafia campaign in the late 1920s. Bellodi is a former partisan, but many of the locals were fascist or Sicilian separatists, so the impact of "the past" on the present is far from straightforward. In Rome, meanwhile, a Mafioso meets with an Honourable Member of Parliament and complains about something Bellodi said: "Has a policeman ever dared to talk so to a man of honour before? He's a communist. Only communists talk like that" (25).

(6) Suspicion of writing, education. The written word, and those who wield it, frighten the Sicilians in *The Day of the Owl*. Carabiniere Sposito is educated, an accountant, and he types up the notes when the brothers are being interviewed. "Sposito had a baby face but the brothers Colasberna and their associates were in holy terror of his presence, the terror of a merciless inquisition, of the black seed of the written word. 'White soil, black seed. Beware of the man who sows it. He never forgets,' says the proverb" (16). When the captain asks the brothers to sign their names, they all claim that they write "very slowly" and with

difficulty. The informer Parriniedu ("Little Priest") mistrusts the law: "To the informer the law was not a rational thing born of reason, but something depending on a man, on the thoughts and the mood of this man here, on the cut he gave himself shaving or a good cup of coffee had has just drunk. To him the law was utterly irrational, created on the spot by those in command . . . It was like a barbed wire entanglement, a wall" (29).

Meanwhile Captain Bellodi frequently alludes to literature and opera. Interviewing Nicolosi's widow, he prides himself on comprehending her dialect because "The Captain had known many Sicilians, during his partisan period, and, later, among the carabinieri. He had also read Giovanni Meli with Francesco Lanza's notes and Ignazio Buttitta with the facing translation by Quasimodo" (39). Homesick, he recalls a verse from an Emilian poet (44). The sergeant-major favors popular fiction. "'Who does he [Bellodi] think he is? Arsène Lupin?' thought the sergeant-major, whose reading days were so far behind him that he mistook burglar for policeman" (41). All of this learning seems pedantic in the context. More important, it is of no avail. Mafia chief Don Mariano Arena tells Bellodi, "I'm not a well-read man: but there's one or two things I do know, and they're enough for me" (101). His implication, borne out at the novel's conclusion, is that whatever the well-read Bellodi knows will prove useless.[22]

The Day of the Owl is a masterpiece, comparable to other classics of regionalism by writers like Thomas Hardy, Willa Cather, and William Faulkner. Regionalist novels vary widely in their use of language—Sciascia's terseness, Faulkner's lushness, Cather's realism—but share the regionalist aesthetic. So this aesthetic must contain its own attractions, over and above the language and imagery that surround it, and over and above the particular plot structure, which can vary from crime story to social comedy to romance to tragedy. The appeal of the regionalist aesthetic, as will be argued in the next section, is the appeal of classical pastoral.

22. Giovanni Mile was an eighteenth-century Sicilian poet. Ignazio Buttitta was a twentieth-century poet who wrote about and in the Sicilian dialect. Lupin was a gentleman burglar in a popular series of French novels.

Literary regionalism of the modern and postmodern period is, in fact, the contemporary manifestation of pastoral, and it attracts and delights its audience through some of the same techniques.

Pastoral

An ancient genre that, in its classical form, strikes many contemporary readers as curiously artificial, pastoral has held a prominent place in European and American literature for at least 2300 years. Ever since the third century BC when Theocritus set down some lines about shepherds and cowherds taking their ease at noon and telling stories about love, it has seemed that the Western world cannot let go of the genre. Pastoral was revived in Rome by Virgil, revived in the Renaissance by Spenser and Shakespeare, revived in the eighteenth century by aristocrats playing shepherdesses, revived in the nineteenth by local-color writers, revived in the twentieth by Tom Stoppard and Philip Roth. What is it about lovesick shepherds?[23]

Not always literally about shepherds, of course, pastorals do feature similar rustic characters—or aristocrats masquerading as rustics. The fundamental feature of the genre is simple characters who express sophisticated ideas. Critic Terry Gifford has usefully sorted out the common uses of the term pastoral into three clusters:

- The historical form of poetry (later drama) begun in classical Greece and Rome, and further developed in the Renaissance, depicting shepherds singing and talking about their work and their loves, against a background of an idealized countryside.
- The broader sense in which "pastoral refers to any literature that describes the country with an implicit or explicit contrast to the urban." The attitude expressed is celebratory, a delight in the natural and the simple.

23. It was during the Renaissance that "pastoral" was designated as a genre. Most commentaries trace the origins of pastoral to Theocritus, a Greek from Sicily, though Theocritus himself called his poetry "bucolic." See Wells (1989, 23–26), for a discussion of the distinction between bucolic and pastoral.

• The critical, pejorative, or simply dismissive term "implying that the pastoral vision is too simplified . . . too complacent to qualify as insight."[24]

Writing in the 1930s, William Empson gave what is still the prevailing account of how pastoral, in the first (strictest) definition, works and why it appeals to people. Empson emphasized the genre's economy, whereby it could speak of many things while appearing to be only herdsmen singing songs. It was "putting the complex into the simple," he contended. "In pastoral you take a limited life and pretend it is the full and normal one." Pastoral comments on social relations by denying social differences. "The essential trick of the old pastoral, which was felt to imply a beautiful relation between rich and poor, was to make simple people express strong feelings (felt as the most universal subject, something fundamentally true about everybody) in learned and fashionable language (so that you wrote about the best subject in the best way.) From seeing the two sorts of people combined like this you thought better of both; the best parts of both were used." The conventions of the genre, especially its praise of the simple life, gives its urban audience a point of comparison—"I am in one way better, in another not so good"—with which to measure their own lives.[25]

24. Gifford (1999). Both quotations from Wells (1989, 2), discuss how Theocritus merged the scholar-poet and the herdsman, putting complex sentiments in the mouths of rustics.

25. Empson ([1935] 1974); "The essential trick" is from pp. 11–12. Empson's pastoral is widely embracing, including Gifford's first and second types plus tales of childhood (e.g., Lewis Carroll) that similarly package sophistication in innocence; writing in the 1930s, Empson even suggests a link between pastoral and the proletarian art, which can be "Covert Pastoral." Paul Alpers (1996) urges a more narrow definition, but again follows the line that the very limitations of its subject allow it to contain vast meanings. "Pastoral makes explicit a certain disproportion between its fictions, conspicuously modest and selective, and the meanings they bear or imply: there is always a suggestion that 'more is meant than meets the ear.'" Answering the question of his title "What is pastoral?" Alpers says the first lines of Theocritus's *Idylls* contain "several features that are regarded as pastoral's defining characteristics: idyllic landscape, landscape as a setting for song, and atmosphere of *otium* [ease, leisure], a conscious attention to art and nature, herdsmen as singers, and, in the account of the gifts, herdsmen as herdsmen." Alpers, like Empson, rejects the view of pastoral as callow, self-indulgent escapism, that is suggested in Gifford's third usage. Alpers (1996, 16, 22).

Although critics from Empson on have vigorously denied that pastoral is "mere escapism," the genre nevertheless does both depict and facilitate a temporary escape. As Andrew Ettin puts it, "the pastoral life is sequestered and protected. The pastoral world will seem, indeed, to be a safely contained and self-contained haven from the hazards of public places and the flow of ordinary time." A pastoral convention has an observing character or characters, including the narrator, temporarily remove themselves from the complex world of town and court to a bucolic retreat. Here they gain both refreshment and wisdom. Then they return, transformed by their temporary retreat, to their previous social worlds. Shakespeare's characters from the Duke's court in *As You Like It* making their retreat to the Forest of Arden, sorting out their amatory and political lives, and then returning to court, is a familiar example.[26]

The retreat-refresh-return movement structures the experience of characters within a pastoral, but—even more important for the present discussion—such a movement *always* structures the experience of the reader (or listener or viewer) of pastoral. Virtually every discussion of the genre emphasizes that the audience for pastoral's simple rural characters is urban and sophisticated. Pastoral, Empson stressed, is a metropolitan genre, not a rural one. It always sets up an implicit contrast between the world of the pastoral characters and the world of their audience. The retreat-and-return (edified, refreshed, wiser, or at least happier) is what this metropolitan audience experiences, and this refreshment is the core of pastoral's appeal.[27]

Pastoral is highly stylized escapism, in the most formal and socially constructive sense. Literary regionalism, even when it

26. Ettin (1984); "the pastoral life" is from p. 13. Ettin noted that the musical comedy *Brigadoon* tweaked this convention by having one outsider decide to remain in the mythical village.

27. "This is the essential paradox of the pastoral: that a retreat to a place apparently without the anxieties of the town, or the court, or the present, actually delivers insights into the culture from which it originates. Pastoral authors are inescapably of their own culture and its preoccupations. Thus the pastoral construct always reveals the preoccupations and tensions of its time" (Gifford 1999, 82).

seems far removed from the pastoral tradition, offers its readers the same opportunity to find entertainment, refreshment, and insight in the countryside. The most common, indeed ubiquitous, vehicle for such rural refreshment is the regional crime story, typically called a "mystery."

The Regional Mystery

Mysteries constitute about one-quarter of all fiction titles published, and probably account for a much higher proportion of what is actually read, or so the bestsellers lists would suggest. Of the several sub-categories, the detective novel, where an individual protagonist uses brains (always) and brawn (often) to solve a crime, is the most common. And a large percentage of these—roughly half of all American and British mysteries—have characteristics that mark them as regional.[28]

In regional mysteries a single, well-developed, and largely realistic setting plays a prominent role. These books differ from thrillers that feature several, usually exotic backdrops, from novels set in non-specific locales like quaint English villages, and from novels set in metropolitan centers like New York City and London. Regional mysteries announce themselves as such, and often come out in series set in the same place and featuring the same detective. They are extremely common.[29]

The key to the American regional mystery is the fourth element in the regional aesthetic, the ongoing tension between

28. A random sample (N=159) of fiction titles published in 1988 listed in the *American Book Publishing Record* included 40 crime novels, or just over 25 percent (Griswold and Hull 1998). A study of the population of Nigerian novels published from the early 1950s through the mid-1990s (N=476) revealed that 22 percent were crime novels (Griswold 2000). Scanning the paperback mysteries available in any bookstore will reveal just how common the regional mysteries are.

29. *Mystery Readers International*, a respected quarterly out of Berkeley, organizes each issue according to theme, and roughly half center on place. For example, the themes for 2001–3 were:

2001 Volume 17. No. 1: **New England Mysteries**; No. 2: Partners in Crime I; No. 3: Partners in Crime II; No. 4: **Oxbridge**.

locals and outsiders. Consider Donald Harstad's *Known Dead*, second of a series featuring a deputy sheriff in rural Iowa. The cover shows a body lying on a plowed field, and over the title is written, "In the American heartland, someone is killing cops." A blurb from the *New York Times* calls Harstad "an author who knows his territory" and another from the *New York Times Book Review* proclaims that "Harstad . . . advances the scary (and perversely entertaining) notion that people are just as cuckoo in the heartland as they are in the Wicked City." Such marketing ploys position the potential buyer as someone *not* from the heartland, someone in fact from the city, for only an urbanite might be "perversely entertained" by this news. The regional mystery, like its pastoral predecessors, is a metropolitan genre.

Known Dead opens with an insider addressing outsiders: "My name is Carl Houseman. I'm a deputy sheriff in Nation County, Iowa . . . I'd like to tell you about the killings we had in our county in the summer of '96, and the subsequent investigation that stood the whole state on its ear. This is my version of what happened. It's the right one." Not only does this blunt statement locate where the action will unfold, but it locates the *truth* as well. As the story unfolds it becomes clear that the federal law enforcers, the supreme outsiders in this type of story, conceal the truth for their own purposes, so the only version you can trust is the local one, Houseman's.

Although Nation County itself is a fiction, Harstad, who was deputy sheriff in Clayton County for twenty-six years, depicts the northeastern Iowa landscape in great detail: rolling roads connect isolated farms and small towns, midsummer heat and humidity, an ominous background of thunder storms and tornado warnings. Interagency weather is stormy as well. Houseman resents the

---

2002 Volume 18. No. 1: **Pacific Northwest Mysteries**; No. 2: Culinary Crime: First Course; No. 3: Culinary Crime: Second Seating; No. 4: **South of the Mason Dixon Line**.

2003 Volume 19. No. 1: **Southern Exposure Redux**; No. 2: Music and Mysteries: Overture; No. 3: Music and Mysteries: Finale; No. 4: **Cool Canadian Crime**.

For the percent of fiction accounted for by mysteries, see Griswold and Hull (1998).

state and federal officials moving in on *his* case. In the third chapter, Iowa's Division of Criminal Investigation (DCI) and its Department of Narcotics Enforcement (DNE) get involved, and Houseman moves to establish who's in charge of his territory. At the crime scene they introduce themselves:

> "Agent Bob Dahl, DNE," said Agent Bob Dahl, interrupting.
> "Deputy Houseman, Investigator," I said. "You helping out here with my case?" It's always a good idea to establish the territorial limits. Right off the bat. Of course I put him at a bit of a disadvantage, because he wouldn't ever say that he was helping me. After all, it was a DNE officer who was dead. But it was in my jurisdiction, and we were going to be fully involved. But he knew that I knew that he was supposed to do just that, and that was what counted. I decided I was going to like him as soon as he answered.
> "I'm helping them," he said, indicating Hester and the rest of the Division of Criminal Investigation team. "But I'll bet they're helping you. I was his partner," he said, obviously referring to Kellerman [the dead officer]" (18).

Whether or not Houseman "likes" someone is roughly a function of how close they are to Nation County. The sheriff's office is a close-knit and effective team. Houseman respects Sheriff Lamar, absent for most of the novel, and there is much affectionate banter between the officers and the good-old-girl dispatchers. Harstad has a respectful, vaguely flirtatious relationship with Hester Gorse, a state DCI officer with whom he has worked before. The FBI is much more problematic, and federal officers who move in are cooperated with but resented because of their vast resources, their tendency to take over, and their unwillingness to reveal information.

Chief among these is Special Agent in Charge Volont, who heads the task force investigating the murders. At a meeting by the Iowa Attorney General's office that includes people from the local (Nation County), state (the Iowa DCI and DNE) and federal (Drug Enforcement Administration [DEA], FBI, the U.S. Attorney's office, IRS) levels, the deputy U.S. Attorney announces that the case may have "international implications," thus falling under the jurisdictions of the DEA and FBI. Houseman thinks:

> "Now, that was bad news. Both agencies having jurisdiction, I mean. DEA and FBI had been competing for the spotlight and the money from the Federal Drug Czar's office for years. Competition in an investigation wasn't a good idea, and I began to get a bit more leery of the whole task force business. Somebody up the line was going to bump the locals right out of business. At least, they would as soon as a good suspect turned up. The good suspect was, by the way, identified by locals in well over 50 percent of the cases" (76–77).

The deputy U.S. Attorney refers to some South American drug cartel connection, which Houseman immediately disbelieves, and introduces Volont. Houseman recognizes his ability: "He was fit, well-groomed, and had a very intelligent look in his eye. You could see a lot of energy burning behind those eyes . . . A bureaucratic aristocrat, so to speak. They'd handed this one to a top agent. It would take somebody like that to get to the bottom of a complex, foreign-involved, murderous, narcotics-oriented case. I knew it sure as hell would be beyond me" (77). This is tongue-in-cheek, but not entirely, for Houseman does worry about being fifty and overweight. The reader knows that it will be Houseman, not the bureaucratic aristocrat, who will solve the case, but throughout the novel his edgy partnership with Volont plays upon cosmopolitan versus provincial know-how.

These inside/outside tensions among the law enforcers parallel those among the villains, libertarian extremists who believe that the Zionist Occupation Government (ZOG) in league with the UN is throwing farmers off their land and suppressing freedom. A Nation County farmer's family is deeply involved, attending neo-Nazi meetings throughout the Midwest and shooting cops and reporters; another local stockpiles weaponry for the coming Armageddon. But the mastermind is an outsider named Gabriel—born in Winnipeg, living in a fortified camp in Idaho—who pops up in various violent actions. After the final shootout leaves many militants shot dead, Volont claims that Gabriel has escaped, but Houseman wonders whether Volont is saying this for his own purposes (to not compromise other federal investigations) or whether it is true. Either way he knows that Volont can manipulate the records so that Gabriel will not be one of the "known dead," a recurring phrase that grates on Houseman.

The shadowy, impressive, effective outsider Gabriel, and the shadowy, impressive, effective outsider Volont both bring trouble to Houseman, the local insider (even his name suggests this). The extremists' paranoia about the ZOG is the vicious counterpart to the Nation County deputy sheriff's virtuous distrust of outside law enforcement agents. But Houseman, the local, has the insight to cut through all the lies. In an epilogue Houseman says that Sheriff Lamar is back and knows "something is very, very wrong"; he plans to tell Lamar everything "before I mail this in" (371). To whom is Houseman sending the story: A lawyer? A journalist? The reader? Although it is not clear, Houseman's desire to get the truth out—"This is my version of what happened. It's the right one."—echoes the militants' conviction that the ZOG/UN has duped everyone else and only they see what's really happening. Here is an echo of Don Mariano's claim for local knowledge, that it's "enough" to know just a few things. And both Houseman and Don Mariano are twentieth-century exemplars of pastoral's complexity-dressed-in-simplicity convention.

While the regional aesthetic always involves some aspect of the relationship between the local and the outside, American crime writers seem to emphasize tension and conflict somewhat more forcefully than do most of their European counterparts. According to Stephen Knight, Sherlock Holmes and other early British crime stories were responses to mobility, both geographic and social. While Holmes lived in London's West End, he ranged throughout southeast England as "the exorcizer of the evils of the newly developed system of London-centered business; a good fairy of mercantile capitalism" in a world where the region was no longer self-sufficient enough to deal with local crimes. Although at first this seems very different from American regional mysteries' assertion of the local capacity to solve local crimes, the English equivalent to inside (good)/outside (bad) is something like tradition (good)/change (bad). One basic mode developed by Agatha Christie opens with "an attractive imaginary regional setting. Soon they will indicate that change is an alarming feature, and then show that those who have internalized and tried to introduce modernization are the villains, those who represent virtues felt to be ancient and durable are both victims and survivors and—most important of all—detectives." Reginald Hill's Dalziel and Pascoe series has "a sense that the region can stand alone and examine itself" that Knight regards as unusual.[30]

Mysteries also raise the more general question of cities, of whether or not an urban crime story (or indeed any urban literature) can qualify as "regional." Crime fiction set in impersonal cities like Los Angeles or London often satisfies the fundamental criterion that place be an integral feature of the story. Such urban mysteries often meet two of the six criteria of the regionalist aesthetic: they depict closely observed physical settings (though more involving the built environment than the natural), and they involve tough local characters of the I've-seen-it-all sort. On the other hand, the other criteria—insider/outsider conflict, reference to the past, educational differences, and of course rurality— are usually absent. Knight argues that London novels are not regional in that they don't see problems as "founded on the historical and social forces of metropolitan power against the rest of the country." Such an interpretation is based on the idea that region is relational; metropolitan novels may be about place, but they are not relational. Admittedly, however, this distinction can

---

30. Knight (1995); "the exorcizer," is from p. 31; "an attractive imaginary regional setting," p. 33. Overall the insider/outsider conflicts, while present, are not quite as sharply drawn in European novels, perhaps because of the difference between federal and centralized political structures. Henning Mankell's detectives operate in Ystad, for example, but rarely chafe at interference from Stockholm; instead, they sometimes get help from the capital. Andrea Camilleri's Sicilian police fight constant internal battles of status and departmental politics, but they largely ignore, and are ignored by, Rome. Reginald Hill's Yorkshire police pay little attention to London, and Scotland Yard does not often interfere.

be hard to maintain, and regions often are happy to claim city authors.[31]

This chapter has argued that although burly Carl Houseman chasing down terrorists in Iowa is no gamboling shepherd, the key features of the regionalist aesthetic—in mysteries or in other literary genres—draw upon those of the pastoral. The reading experience is parallel as well. Readers of regionalism escape from their metropolitan world, retreating into a countryside of formal, insider/outsider conventions. There they are refreshed, entertained, and enlightened. Afterward they return to the city, to the messy and unresolved world of real life. While escape is commonly said to be one of the pleasures of reading, it is less often remarked that it is an escape *to somewhere*. The regional aesthetic confirms the experience of those readers who are from the region itself. More important, it offers the retreat/return movement to that much larger group of readers who are *not* native to the region, readers whose experience is not confirmed but extended by regional literature.

These are the members of the reading class. To understand the robust appeal of literary regionalism, our next task must be to understand the makeup and motivations of readers in general and the reading class in particular. This is the subject of the following chapter.

31. Knight (1995, 42).

The Reading Class

WITH TERENCE EMMETT MCDONNELL AND
NATHAN WRIGHT[1]

Regional culture is peculiarly dependent on readers for its very existence. The demand for place-specific mysteries, poetry, cookbooks, travel guides, magazines, and local newspapers sustains it. If no one read crime novels, there would still be crime; if there were no romance-novel fans, people would still discover love. Mapping the invisible landscape, on the other hand, requires words, and if the knowledge of place culture is to extend beyond the strictly local, it requires print. Take away readers, take away the apparatus of printing and distributing and reading about and writing about place, and regionalism atrophies. It follows, therefore, that the prospects for regionalism depend on the prospects for reading.

Today, the prospects for reading are not bright. Most people in advanced industrial and post-industrial countries are not and will not be readers. Although they read for work and for information, routinely and matter-of-factly, they entertain themselves with electronic media. Only a few get lost in a book, turn to newspapers

---

1. Portions of this chapter come from Griswold, McDonnell, and Wright (2005). For the reading class and reading culture, see Griswold (2001).

for news and magazines for leisure, and are called "readers" by their family and friends.

These few constitute the reading class. The reading class consists of those people who read for entertainment constantly. These are the folks who always have a book going, who never travel without something to read, who have print materials scattered in every room of their houses. This reading class is and will be modest in size but immense in cultural influence. And one of its impacts is the support and cultivation of regionalism.

Every society that has writing has a reading class, but not everyone who can read is a member. A reading class has a stable set of characteristics that include its human capital (education), its economic capital (wealth, income, occupational positions), its social capital (networks of personal connections), its demographic characteristics (gender, age, religion, ethnic composition), and—the defining and non-economic characteristic—its cultural practices. A reading class is not the same thing as a reading culture. A reading class is a social formation, while a reading culture is a society where reading is expected, valued, and common. All societies with written language have a reading class but few have a reading culture.

Readers have been a privileged minority throughout most of human history. Although written records and communications became established in certain institutional niches, most people occupied themselves with basic tasks—farming and hunting, tending children, fighting—for which reading and writing were not much help. Reading was mainly useful for activities involving coordination and memory—administration, trade, organized religion—and early readers were the people involved in these activities: rulers and their staffs, merchants, priests. Thus even in so-called literate societies, the vast majority, including almost all women, almost all rural people, and most slaves, did not read, and their lives were no worse off for it.

Only during the past three centuries, and only in northwest Europe, North America, Japan, and a few cities elsewhere, did reading become routine. Only in the heyday of the Industrial Revolution did reading become a common leisure-time activity. Only where industrialism began to give way to the postindustrial, information society did reading become necessary for holding a good job, thereby marking the difference between the skilled and the unskilled. Yet despite its historical novelty and uneven distribution, today the ability to read is considered to be a fundamental human right.[2]

To understand the prospects for regionalism requires taking a close look at reading and readers. The burden of this chapter is to assess where reading currently stands and where it is headed.

Readers in the Past

Histories of readers and reading have been told in three ways. First, the history of literacy, associated with modernization theories of the mid-twentieth century, asks who could read, how people learned to read, and what difference literacy made to socioeconomic development. Second, the history of the book, which arose in the 1970s, asks about the production and distribution of books as material objects. And finally the history of reading, which spun off from the history of the book in the 1990s, asks who owned or otherwise had access to written materials, and how they read and interpreted them. All three contribute to a sociological understanding of reading's trajectory.[3]

2. Article 26 of the Universal Declaration of Human Rights, adopted and proclaimed by General Assembly resolution 217 A (III) of 10 December 1948: "(1) Everyone has the right to education. Education shall be free, at least in the elementary and fundamental stages. Elementary education shall be compulsory . . . " Literacy gained further support in 1959 when the Declaration of the Rights of the Child proclaimed by General Assembly resolution 1386 (XIV) of 20 November 1959 proclaimed: "Principle 7: The child is entitled to receive education, which shall be free and compulsory, at least in the elementary stages. He shall be given an education which will promote his general culture and enable him, on a basis of equal opportunity, to develop his abilities, his individual judgment, and his sense of moral and social responsibility, and to become a useful member of society." Elementary education means basic literacy and numeracy.

3. The classic works in the history of literacy are Cippola (1969) and Goody (1968, 1977). For the history of the book, see the overview by Robert Darnton (1990, ch. 7). For the history of reading, see Cavallo and Chartier (1999), Andersen and Sauer (2002), Amtower (2000), and Coleman (1996). Darnton (1990, ch. 9) thinks the history of the book is broadening into a history of reading, the former seeing books as material objects,

The modernization thesis held mass literacy to be one of the prerequisites for a society making the transition from tradition to modernity. According to this theory, even advanced countries had "backwards" groups (e.g., African Americans) and regions (e.g., southern Italy) characterized by low rates of education and economic disadvantage. Literacy was part of a package of remedies that would bring such groups and regions up to speed. People assumed that the "consequences of literacy," to use the title of an influential essay, were both profound and beneficial: literacy was a permanent condition, it required schools, it produced individual mobility and reduced social inequality, and it was politically and ideologically neutral.[4]

While claims of its capacity to undo social injustices were no doubt extravagant, literacy remains a fundamental goal for most individuals and for all countries. And while people can use written materials without being able to read them—use them as interior decorations, as fetishes, as symbols, as sacred objects, as doorstops—reading requires literacy. Any six-year-old knows this as she scornfully informs her younger brother "You're not *reading*, you're just looking at the pictures." So a sociological look at reading must begin with a historical look at literacy.

The first writing system was cuneiform, which appeared in the city-states of Sumer, in southern Mesopotamia, in the fourth millennium BC. Sumerians wrote on clay tablets to record commercial transactions, business and personal communications, hymns,

the latter as part of a system involving readers, writers, technologies, publishers, editors, texts, booksellers, reviewers, political regimes, and educational and religious institutions.

4. In "The Consequences of Literacy," Jack Goody and Ian Watt (1968) drew a sharp line between oral societies, whose cultures were homeostatic, reliant on memory to confirm existing social arrangements, and literate societies, whose cultures could deal with abstract thought and recognized a distinction between myth and history. History, logic, critical thinking, and democracy were among the consequences of literacy, as was individualism, skepticism, stratification based on what one had read, and the alienation that comes from individuals' inability to master the entirety of their culture. Harvey Graff (1987, 264) has tried to debunk the "literacy myth" linking literacy, schooling, modernization, democracy, and individual social mobility. He regards nineteenth-century advances in schooling as "the process of recreating cultural hegemony," inducting the working class into the moral community required by industrial capitalism.

magic, and, in the second millennium, the *Epic of Gilgamesh*. From that time on, traders, cultural leaders, and city folks have always been first to read and write. In most so-called literate societies a few urban men involved in commerce or holding political or religious offices could read, but not the population as a whole. Imperial Rome is regarded as literate, for example, but less than a third of Roman men and a tenth of the women could read.[5]

To be able to record sales and accounts, to able to interpret signs and notices, is to be literate, but these activities are not usually regarded as reading. Early writing preserved information, and people could consult these texts. A change came in the late fifth century BC, when books began to be designed not just to preserve texts but also to be read. Vases from Greece and the Hellenistic world are decorated with pictures suggesting that people read socially, while carrying on conversations or watching entertainments. Most reading was oral, with multiple listeners. Private libraries appeared, although these may have been collections primarily for display.[6]

The third and second centuries BC saw an expansion of reading and books. Greek books flooded into Rome as war booty, and wealthy Romans built private libraries to house them. Such libraries, many opening onto gardens, were gathering places for elite coteries. Some public libraries were established as well; these were still essentially scholarly in that "although they were open to anyone, in reality they were frequented by a reading public from the middle-to-high levels of society—that is, roughly the same persons who had access to private libraries" (in other words, the reading class). Roman readers benefited from a gradual replacement

5. The *Gilgamesh* epic that we have today comes from a copy made for the library of Ashurbanipal, an Assyrian king in about 600 BC, but fragments from tablets come from between 1300 and 1000 BC, and it is believed that the oral versions of the hero's tale are much older. If a historical Gilgamesh existed, and there is disagreement over this, he may have reigned around 2600 BC. For estimates of Greek and Roman literacy, see Harris (1989).

6. This section relies on the invaluable history of reading in the West compiled by Cavallo and Chartier (1999). The discussion of Greece and Rome also draws on Harris (1989).

of rolls (*volumina*) by the more manageable codex format. Despite such developments, it is misleading to think of Rome and Roman cities as being reading cultures. Rome had a literate elite, a small but active reading class, and it had institutions that supported reading and the possession and discussion of books. There was public reading in the forum and there was graffiti on the walls. Most people were not literate, however, and only a few read for pleasure or instruction.[7]

Following the collapse of the Roman Empire, reading and writing in Europe was kept alive in the monasteries. Reading was not just something done by people who devoted their lives to sacred things; reading itself was sacred. Article 38 of the Rule of Saint Benedict specified that "At the mealtime of the brothers there should always be reading . . . And there shall be the greatest silence at table, so that no whispering or any voice save the reader's may be heard." Monastic authorities selected the readings, and forbade private interpretations.[8]

While Byzantium continued practices from the classical past, for example reading aloud and using rolls instead of codices, the Latin West saw changes. Reading moved inside, from gardens, porticos, and public squares, to "the confined spaces of churches, monks' cells, refectories, cloisters, religious schools, and on occasion, courts." Reading aloud began to give way to silent or mumbled reading, which was not common until the tenth century. Writing became easier to comprehend quickly once manuscripts began to separate words and include punctuation. While the technologies of monastic reading and writing were utterly different from what was to come, the actual practices of reading—silent visual inspection leading to private mental apprehension of the text—were roughly the same as today.[9]

---

7. Cavallo and Chartier (1999, 13–14).

8. Rule of Saint Benedict quoted in Manguel (1996, 114–16).

9. During the latter days of the Roman Empire, Christians favored the codex because it was easier to conceal it under their clothing, and the format took hold. Manguel (1996, 41–53) describes the centuries-long development of silent reading. "The confined spaces . . . " quotation is from Cavallo and Chartier (1999, 16).

Early readers, whether Assyrian merchants writing up receipts, wealthy Romans entertaining their friends, or cloistered monks copying scripture, constituted an exceedingly thin layer of society. This began to change during the late Middle Ages, from the eleventh through the fourteenth centuries, as literacy started moving out of the monasteries and into the growing cities. Technical changes—dividing pages into columns, breaking up texts into sections, using abbreviations—made reading easier. A new type of reading emerged: reading for content. The book became:

> an object to be used . . . a source from which to draw knowledge (or specific bits of knowledge), rather than a depository for things to ruminate (*ruminare*) or simply an object to be kept . . . What had formerly been total, intensive and repetitive reading of a limited number of books gave way to scattered reading of many books. Moreover, this occurred in an age—the age of scholasticism—characterized by an immense increase in the number of written texts and by a demand for a broad but fragmentary knowledge.[10]

These changes in reading—from oral to silent, from collecting texts to using them, from libraries that accumulated books to libraries that facilitated their reading (with catalogs and a new rule: no talking), from intensive reading of the monasteries to the more extensive reading of scholars—took place well before Gutenberg. In the thirteenth century literacy spread among the laity, and vernacular books began to appear. Aristocrats collected books and reading became popular among courtiers. More than a millennium after the gatherings in the Roman gardens, people again displayed their reading to gain social status.[11]

10. Cavallo and Chartier (1999, 18–19).

11. The historical dichotomy between intensive and extensive reading has been much debated. It involves two basic ideas: First, under some reading cultures people read the same text over and over, the typical example being monks poring over scripture, while under other reading cultures people read more superficially and from a wide variety of materials. Second, reading has undergone a shift from the first, intensive mode to the second, extensive mode. The German historian Rolf Engelsing, who originated the dichotomy, saw this shift taking place in the late eighteenth century, while other

Printing, launched in mid-fifteenth century with Gutenberg's movable-type technology, set off revolutionary social change. Historian Elizabeth Eisenstein, for example, has attributed both the Reformation and the growth of the scientific method to print. A second time of changes came in the eighteenth century with the commercialization and then industrialization of printing. This revolution was not simply another move toward ever more extensive reading (novels were read intensively, for example), but a development that put reading materials firmly in the hands of the urban middle classes. The late eighteenth century saw a "rage for reading" characterized by the "growth in book production, which tripled or quadrupled between the beginning of the century and the 1780s, the rapid multiplication of newspapers, the triumph of small book formats, lower book prices brought about by pirated editions and the proliferation of institutions (reading societies and lending libraries) that made it possible to read books and periodicals without having to buy them."[12]

By the beginning of the nineteenth century, modern reading practices were set. Most (though by no means all) reading was secular, was utilitarian or for entertainment, and was done in private. Modern reading involved news and public affairs, educational and religious material, narrative fiction, and business and personal communications. Modern readers tended to be Protestant, from the North Atlantic, middle class or associated with it—domestic servants read a lot—and urban. Men read earliest, but reading had spread among women, especially in Protestant countries where reading the Bible and educating the children both encouraged it.

---

scholars have placed in much earlier, either with the coming of print (Eisenstein 1979) or even earlier in the late Middle Ages, when reading practices of scholasticism had replaced monasticism (Cavallo and Chartier 1999). See Darnton (1990), esp. 132–34, for a discussion of this dichotomy.

12. See Eistenstein (1979). The quoted description of the late eighteenth century "rage for reading" comes from Cavallo and Chartier (1999, 26). They maintain, contrary to Eisenstein's widely accepted thesis, that the initial reading revolution actually predated Gutenberg's technological advances.

The nineteenth and twentieth centuries extended the basic pattern. In Britain "[t]he late Victorian period ushered in an unprecedented phenomenon, a mass reading public . . . this was both the first and the *only* mass literary age." Reading moved to the working class, to the south and east of Europe, to the countryside, to women, to minority groups, to European colonies. Reading became firmly established in Asian cities, and everywhere in Japan. Reading became the norm throughout Latin America. Even in many countries of sub-Saharan Africa and the Arab world, more and more people could read. By the mid-twentieth century virtually everyone in the developed world and many city dwellers of the less developed world could read.[13]

Readers Today

In the West, in Japan, and in urban centers worldwide, just about everyone reads. Even illiterates in cities routinely decode billboards and bus schedules. While rural areas of the developing world lag, here the goal of universal literacy has become less a question of whether it is possible and more a question of when it will be achieved.

UNESCO (United Nations Educational, Scientific and Cultural Organization) offers a comparative view, and while such statistics must be taken with a chunk of salt—different countries measure literacy differently, and governments have incentives to inflate literacy figures—they indicate some general patterns. In places where reading is not universal, women invariably have lower rates of literacy than men do; the higher the overall literacy rate is, the smaller the gender gap. At the regional level, South Asia has the lowest overall literacy (58.5%), which breaks down

---

13. Cipolla (1969) provides a general account, firmly within the modernization paradigm, of the historical relationship between literacy and development in the West. Rose (2001) examines one particular instance of this relationship, that of nineteenth-century Britain. He argues that literacy made working people not simply "modern" but revolutionary in their thinking. "The late Victorian . . ." quotation is from Waller 2006, 3). For the period leading up to this Victorian heyday, see St. Clair (2004).

into rates of 71.1% for men and 45.3% for women. Northern and sub-Saharan Africa show similar patterns. But South-Eastern Asia has a higher overall literacy rate (89.2%) and less of a gender gap (92.8% of men and 85.7% of women can read). Eastern Asia is similar, and in Latin America, although the literacy rate (89.3%) is almost identical to that of Southeast Asia, the gender gap has largely disappeared.[14]

Reading and the reading habits of Europeans and North Americans have been surveyed for decades. How a question is worded can have a powerful effect on how it is answered, so comparisons over time and space cannot be taken too seriously. Nevertheless, recent snapshots give some sense of reading's dimensions.

Most Americans and Europeans read during their leisure time. According to the 1994 International Adult Literacy Survey of seven advanced economies (Canada, Germany, Netherlands, Poland, Sweden, Switzerland, United States), almost everyone reads a newspaper at least once a week. Reading books is less common: "Fewer than 40% of respondents in any country reported reading books daily; about 66% at least once a month." A 2001 Gallup poll finds that Americans report spending an average of over a half hour reading magazines, close to three-quarters of an hour reading newspapers, and over an hour reading books during a "normal day," but these averages are skewed by the heavy readers. In 1998, when the General Social Survey asked if respondents had "read novels, short stories, poems, or plays, other than those required by work or school" during the past twelve months, 70 percent reported that they had. While these survey statistics are hard to reconcile (do half of American adults read books every day or don't they?), the basic picture is clear: in advanced countries, people read a lot.[15]

---

14. UNESCO (2004a, 2004b). These tables can be found at the UNESCO Institute for Statistics website on "Literacy Statistics": http://www.uis.unesco.org/ev .php?URL_ID=5204&URL_DO=DO_TOPIC&URL_SECTION=201."

15. OECD and Statistics Canada (1994); the quotation ("Fewer than 40%...") is from p. 105. According to Gallup Poll (2001, questions 35c–e), only 18.99% of Americans say they spend no time reading newspapers during a normal day, 24.81% devote no time

People worry that they should be reading more—nine out of ten are convinced that reading is "a good use of your time"—and they don't make the excuse that reading is "too hard to do." They expect to read more in the future, particularly more materials that will educate or improve them like nonfiction books, newspapers, and the Bible. A British survey finds that 80 percent of the respondents actually believe they are reading the same or even more than they did five years earlier.[16]

Everywhere, reading depends on education. A twenty-country survey concludes, "Formal educational attainment is the main determinant of literacy proficiency. For 17 of the 20 countries it is both the first and the strongest predictor." Holding schooling constant, reading is associated with:

---

to books, and 33.33% don't read magazines. About a third of Americans spend an hour reading the newspaper, with 6.89% spending over two hours; a quarter spend an hour or more reading magazines. Books consume more time: 25.33% of people spend one hour, 14.46% spend two hours, and 11.31% spend three hours or more with books.= See also General Social Survey (1998) in the reference list for this volume.

16. According to the Gallup Poll (2003a), over half of all Americans (53.91%) feel they spend too little time reading (question 16g). An earlier survey found that almost three-quarters of people felt they spent too little time reading books for pleasure and recreation, while 62.27% felt they spend too little time reading books for work and school (Gallup Poll 1990; questions 22d–e). When that same survey asked "Do you think you'll find yourself reading more in the months and years ahead, reading less, or is the amount of reading you do probably going to stay the same?" 45% said more, 3% less, 51% said the same (question 24). People fret that they don't read as many books as they used to (question 32b).

When Gallup asked, "Over the next five years, will you be spending more time, less time, or about the same amount of time" reading different materials in 1991, 37.33% expected to read the Bible more (11.03% expected to read it less) and 33.55% planned to read more nonfiction (15.20% expected to read less). On the other hand, for fiction and for religious books other than the Bible, the percents expecting to read more and expecting to read less were about the same, about 20% in each case. Along similar lines, there was a larger difference in the number who expected to read the newspaper more versus less (30.17% thought they would read it more, and only 7.08% less) than in the number for magazines (23.26% expected to do more magazine reading, 16.185 less). Newspapers, when compared to magazines, are probably regarded as having a higher ratio of enlightenment to entertainment (Gallup Poll 1991).

The "good use of your time" question is from Gallup Poll (1990, question 23). The "too hard to do" excuse is from the same (question 48b). The British survey referred to is Book Marketing Ltd. (2000, 9).

- Income and/or wealth (affluent people read more, although not all affluent groups are heavy readers)
- Race and ethnicity (the racial/ethnic configuration varies from country to country)
- Gender (women read more than men)
- Place of residence (reading is an urban or suburban practice).[17]

Historically, reading has been a metropolitan phenomenon. Cities that were commercial or administrative centers—Shanghai, Lagos, Moscow—have lead their respective countries in the literacy and print revolutions, while purely industrial cities have lagged behind others because they drew a labor force that did not necessarily need to be literate. Men gain literacy first, but when this difference evens out, women read more.[18]

Another universal pattern: no sooner does a popular reading culture get established than commentators start worrying about the decline of reading. Headlines from China's *People's Daily* sound the alarm: "Chinese People Read Less," according to a new survey. Educated Africans bemoan that the reading cultures of the late colonial and early independence period are decaying. Such concerns, regardless of their basis in reality, attest to the immense value societies place on reading.[19]

Sometimes religious or ethnic minorities lead the rest of the population in reading, and sometimes they lag. Historically, Protestants were early and avid readers because of the Reformation's emphasis on direct access to the Bible. In many European countries, Jews have read more than their countrymen. In countries with both Muslim and non-Muslim populations, the Muslims

17. "Formal education . . . ": OECD and Statistics Canada (2000, 58). Other sources for readers' demographic characteristics include Book Marketing Ltd. (2000); National Endowment for the Arts (2004a); see also Cushman, Veal, and Zuzanek (1996) for the universality of the gender difference. For a summary of demographic findings, see Ross, McKechnie, and Rothbauer (2006, ch. 4).

18. See Perry Link (1981) for the growth of reading in Shanghai; Griswold (2000) for Lagos; Brooks (1985) for Moscow; and Furet and Ozouf (1982) for data on commercial versus industrial cities.

19. "Chinese People Read Less" is from the *People's Daily Online* (2004). For concerns of educated Africans, see Griswold (2000).

may read less and confine their attention to religious texts rather than secular material like fiction. In the United States, race and ethnicity have a strong impact on reading. In 2004, the National Endowment for the Arts found that 26 percent of Hispanics, 37 percent of African Americans, and 51 percent of white Americans read literature (defined as novels, short stories, poetry, and plays). African Americans and Hispanics read less regardless of income or education.[20]

Readers start early. Two-thirds of Americans say they started reading by age seven. Parents read to their children as early as during their first year of life, and often continue well after when the children are reading by themselves.[21]

A large survey of American children's media habits found children averaging forty-five minutes a day in recreational reading. Most kids—between 80 and 90 percent—read at least some every day, and close to half read more than thirty minutes a day. Recreational reading drops in the late teen years, though by then most are at least glancing at newspapers. Comparing their survey with earlier research, Roberts and Foehr conclude "the proportion of U.S. children and adolescents who do so [read newspapers] has remained fairly constant over past 50 years." Overall young people's reading time declines with age, and this decline is entirely from a drop in reading books.

> As youngsters move from elementary school into middle and high school, they are typically asked to engage in a good deal more school-related reading than was formerly the case, a factor that probably reduces both desire and time to read outside school. In addition, during late adolescence, myriad additional activities vie for young people's time—sports, extracurricular activities, social events, earning a driver's

---

20. The reading statistics come from National Endowment for the Arts (2004a, 11, table 9). A few years earlier the same pattern was found by DiMaggio and Ostrower (1992). The growth of African American "chick lit" suggests that Black women's reading is picking up; see Lee (2004).

21. Gallup Poll (1990). The finding that two-thirds start by age seven comes from question 42, and the findings about parental reading come from questions 44 and 48.

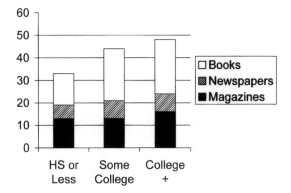

FIGURE 4. Daily reading (youth) by parental education

license, part-time jobs, dating... leisure time print exposure is also related to available time, and available time is related to age.[22]

Parents' education strongly influences children's "print exposure," especially to books (fig. 4). Both the physical environments (books and newspapers in the home, magazine subscriptions, family income) and social environments (parents' education, television orientation, which as always has a negative impact on reading) can encourage or discourage children's reading, with the social environment being the more powerful.[23]

In contrast to some research and to widespread belief, Roberts and Foehr conclude that "there is little evidence that young people's leisure reading has changed much over the past half-century... If anything, the averages we found are a bit higher than those that seem to have held for some time. Perhaps the increasing number of magazines aimed at children and adolescents and such children's book phenomena as the recent Harry Potter craze

22. Roberts and Foehr (2004, 98, table 6.1). "The proportion..." is from p. 99. "As youngsters move..." is from pp. 100–101.

23. Children whose parents have a high school education or less average 33 minutes of reading a day (only 14 of which go to reading books); those whose parents have some college education average 43 minutes of reading a day (23 of which go to books); and those whose parents have a college degree average 49 minutes (24 of which go to books). Roberts and Foehr (2004, 103 (figure 6.3).

may be helping reading gain a bit." Similarly, a 1994 survey of 8,000 English children found that since 1971, reading for most categories of children had either increased or remained steady. Although such reports are encouraging, one cannot be too sanguine about the constancy of young people's reading habits. The Roberts and Foehr survey was conducted in 1999, and Internet behavior has changed enormously since then. Instant messaging and downloading MP3s may be cutting further into the leisure time of young people. And the English survey took place well before the impact of the Internet had made itself felt. Virtually all teachers and parents are convinced that "kids read less these days."[24]

Girls everywhere are the better readers. If girls receive equal education (not the case in many African and Muslim countries), they read both more and more effectively than boys. Research comparing children's reading in thirty-two countries showed girls lead boys consistently. A British survey indicates that gender differences appear early. When the survey asked very young children (ages 4–7) "How often do you read story books?" 67.6 percent of girls but only 55.5 percent of boys responded "very often" or "often"; by ages 7–11 the responses had gone up for both, but the gender difference remained. Reading then declined in the early teen years, but the decline in boys' reading was sharper.[25]

Many studies suggest that leisure reading is declining overall. Literature has always been a minority pastime—a study of "literary reading" in the early 1990s showed that only a small fraction of the adult population read any serious fiction, poetry, or drama—and today even middlebrow and light reading may be giving way to other forms of entertainment. A comprehensive monograph from the National Endowment for the Arts reporting on reading

24. Roberts and Foehr (2004, 112). Hall and Coles (1999) report the findings of the English survey.

25. The thirty-two-country study is reported in Wagemaker (1996), esp. 34, table 7. The British study is reported in Children's Literature Research Centre (1996); see p. 60 for the percents quoted. Another survey of English children suggested that reading had increased significantly for all 10-year-olds and for 12-year-old girls between 1971 and 1994, while reading for 14-year-old boys had decreased significantly (Hall and Coles 1999).

surveys conducted by the U.S. Census Bureau in 1982, 1992, and 2002 showed a steady decline in reading, especially the reading of literature and especially among young adults. The numbers are dismal. In 1982 56.9% of Americans read literature, by 1992 the figure had dropped to 54%, and in 2002 it was at 46.7%. The decline has taken place for all races, both sexes, all educational levels, and all age groups, with young adults showing the steepest decline.[26]

Knulst and Kraaycamp reach a similar conclusion in the Netherlands: survey data from 1955 to 1995 shows a steady drop in leisure reading, which they attribute to television's competition for free time. Younger cohorts read less and, unlike earlier generations, they don't increase their reading as they age. While the percentage of Dutch who read books during the week declined, those people who *did* read books and newspapers in 1995 spent more time reading than did the larger group of readers in earlier decades. "This demonstrates that especially newspaper and book readers who spent relatively little time reading have dropped out" (137). The same concentration effect is suggested in the National Endowment for the Arts (NEA) study: about one in six people are "frequent" (12–49 books per year) or "avid" (over 50 books per year) readers. It appears that it is the more casual reading by occasional readers, not the extensive reading by avid readers, that is atrophying.[27]

Plausible as the decline of reading thesis seems, it is not uncontested. A recent review of the research challenges the pessimistic conclusions of the NEA study. Ross, McKechnie, and Rothbauer conclude that reading is holding steady, including among young people, and that the Internet and electronic media are

26. National Endowment for the Arts (2004a); for earlier evidence of the small proportion of readers who do "literary reading"—poetry, drama, serious fiction—see Zill and Winglee (1990).

27. Knulst and Kraaykamp (1997, 1998); the quotation beginning "This demonstrates . . ." comes from 1997, 137. For the discussion of light, moderate, frequent, and avid readers, as measured in the 2002 *Survey of Public Participation in the Arts,* see National Endowment for the Arts (2004a, 4–5).

not having a negative impact. "Surveys of reading conducted in various high-income countries over the past fifty years have repeatedly found that about 80 to 90 percent of the population reads *something;* 50 to 60 percent of the population reads books as a chosen leisure activity; and 10 to 15 percent of the population are avid readers, who borrow and buy the lion's share of books, magazines, newspapers, and other media consumed."[28] A Canadian study points out that the NEA finding of an abrupt drop in American reading from 1992 to 2002 might have been a post-9/11 effect, the survey taken in "a period during which the audience for electronic media was exceptionally high, which could have distorted the survey results."[29]

Reading of printed materials is certainly under assault, and some decline, especially among the less committed readers, seems inevitable. Newspaper reading of print editions is in trouble. Different surveys tell different stories, but it is safe to say that for some people, the intense competition for leisure time offered by other activities is bound to erode the position that reading books for pleasure once held.[30]

How People Read

Everybody either reads or wants to be able to read. Any "decline of reading" does not mean fewer people read when necessary—clearly more people read now than ever before—but that fewer people engage in extended leisure reading of printed materials, especially books or "serious literature." Reading is essential for most jobs in the developed world, as unskilled manufacturing jobs move offshore, and despite some early expectations to the contrary, it is all but essential for using the Internet. In other words, there is Reading (sitting down with a book) and then there is reading (getting on with one's life in a text-saturated world).

---

28. Ross, McKechnie, and Rothbauer (2006); quote from 17–18.
29. *Reading and Buying Books for Pleasure* (2005); quote from p. 4, note 1.
30. "Who Killed the Newspaper?" in the *Economist* (August 24, 2006) offers an overview of the impact of the Internet on the newspaper business.

This raises the question of not *who* reads but *how?* Under what circumstances do people who *can* read actually *do so?* Put this way, the question recognizes reading to be both social and physical, "an external, social act, performed by people in interaction and in a particular context."[31]

For example, not all places are equally suited for leisure reading. Reading is easy in coffee houses, under baobab trees, in gardens, at private clubs, in public reading rooms, in department store women's lounges, in locker rooms, in libraries, in beauty and barber shops, in restaurants, at kitchen tables, in bathtubs, on toilets, in bed, and on most types of public or private transportation. It is more difficult to read in offices, in shops, in church, on horseback, or while walking down the street, although plenty of reading has been done in all of these places. And it is almost impossible to read while working on an assembly line, driving, running, or taking a shower, although listening to books on tape, which can accompany all of these, blurs the distinction. In fact, surprisingly few situations are not suitable for reading: swimming, having sex, and sleeping come to mind. Certain places are understood to be especially suited to certain reading materials; beach books, airplane reading, and the magazines in doctor's offices are familiar examples. Other places are not reader friendly. People rarely read in public, formal areas like lobbies, or similar domestic spaces like front halls.

Time, as well as space, organizes people's reading. Most newspaper readers like them in the morning. Detective novels are for nighttime. Magazines are good for short intervals: waiting rooms, kitchens, bathrooms. Women with families use reading to achieve some respite, deploying the most feminine (and denigrated) of genres, the romance novel, to claim some time off. People who

---

31. Literacy itself is neither only a set of mental skills nor only a social performance. It is "a concept that embraces the cultural resources of a literate tradition—including the writing system(s) of this tradition—and the ensemble of abilities necessary to exploit these cultural resources" (Brockmeier, Wang, and Olson 2002, 11). "An external, social act . . ." is from Cherland (1994, 5). See also Wagner, Venezky, and Street (1999), esp. essays by Finnegan and Heath.

are reading at the wrong time—e.g., when someone is trying
to talk with them—will be criticized for "having your nose in a
book." Reading can be socially out of sync; a professor I know
who likes to save his *New York Times* for after work gets irritated
at colleagues who insist on discussing articles at lunch.³²

While much reading is done in private spaces, the very structure of privacy is social. In Japan, during the Heian period (794–
1185), the women at court, sequestered in luxury but bored to dis-
traction, entertained themselves with stories, creating a women's
vernacular language in the process. Lady Murasaki's *The Tale
of Genji*, completed in the early eleventh century, comes from
this world: rich in psychological perspicacity, written and read
in intimate space. Reading in feminine interior spaces persists in
Muslim societies that practice purdah.

The private space where the greatest amount of leisure reading takes place is the bed. Children are read to before bedtime or
naps; this both quiets them down and establishes the book-bed
connection. Being in one's bed is usually being "not at work"
by definition (even prostitutes try to have a different bed for
sleeping from the bed in which they work), so leisure activities—
reading, watching television, cuddling—are possible. Temporal
boundaries reinforce spatial ones. Alberto Manguel offers a lyri-
cal account:

> I too read in bed. In the long succession of beds in which I spent the
> nights of my childhood, in strange hotel rooms where the lights of
> passing cars swept eerily across the ceiling, in houses whose smells
> and sounds were unfamiliar to me, in summer cottages sticky with
> sea spray or where the mountain air was so dry that a steaming basin
> of eucalyptus water was placed by my side to help me breathe, the
> combination of bed and book granted me a sort of home which I
> knew I could go back to, night after night, under whichever skies.
> No one would call out and ask me to do this or that; my body
> was immobile, under the sheets. What took place, took place in the

32. For the romance readers, see Radway (1991).

book, and I was the story's teller. Life happened because I turned the pages.[33]

In addition to its emphasis on context, the research on how people read—reading as a practice rather than a capacity—has emphasized two things. First, it holds that *reading is constant:* regardless of whether they ever sit down with a book, people read all the time as they pursue their everyday activities. Second it holds that *reading is collective:* not only do people read together, not only do people discuss what they have read, but even individual reading is shaped by collective memberships.

Contexts, everyday needs, and collective life shape reading practices at the micro level of the household (Mommy's quiet time is respected except when a kid gets hurt) and the macro level of the society (war derails a generation's reading proficiency). Contexts first and foremost involve the material and institutional circumstances of reading: whether people are literate; whether they have access to print materials, free time, and sufficient light; whether they read for school, for work, for leisure; whether their buses are comfortable or packed; whether their electricity is reliable; whether they have long, dark winters (the Nordic countries have the world's highest reading rates). The idea of context goes beyond such conditions to include the geopolitical context, the gender context, and even the literacy context itself.[34]

In her reconstruction of two literacy environments, Deborah Brandt compared Genna (born 1898) and her great-grandson Michael (born 1981):

> In the sparse setting of Genna May's prairie farmhouse, paper, hard to come by, was reserved for her father's church work [she used

33. Manguel (1996, 150–51). He vividly describes the history of reading in bed—those who insisted on its pleasures, those who warned against it—on pp. 149–61.

34. The conception of literacy as a network of practices is discussed in Fernandez (2001). For material and institutional circumstance see Griswold (2000). The impact of the Cold War on reading is discussed in Anghelescu and Poulain (2001). For gender, there is a wealth of literature that shows how reading conforms to and reproduces gender roles, including Cherland (1994); Currie (1999); Roberts and Foehr (2004); Barton and Hamilton (1998, ch. 10).

a slate]. In Michael May's print-clutter suburban ranch home, his parents introduced him to writing and reading amid the background chatter of network television. For members of the community in which Genna May grew up, the ability to write the words of everyday life often marked the end of formal schooling, whereas for Michael May, these same experiences served as a preparation for kindergarten.

Genna and her great-grandson both became readers, but in radically different contexts, so their reading skills meant very different things. Genna's reading was a ticket to upward social mobility, while so far Michael's reading is merely an indication of normal development.[35]

As part of their ethnographic study of a working-class neighborhood in Lancaster, England, David Barton and Mary Hamilton examined the everyday literacy practices of four individuals:

- Harry, a retired fireman, is a widower and WWII veteran. He reads a lot, especially newspapers and histories of the second World War, and every week he and an old friend discuss their reading over tea. Scorning novels, Harry prefers "the real authentic thing," e.g., war memoirs. He uses literacy to make sense of his life.
- Shirley is a middle-aged mother and a community activist. She writes the newsletter for area residents, and fires off letters to the local schools about their treatment of dyslexic children. Shirley uses her literacy to get things done.
- June, in her early forties, lives a "local life." Expressing no interest in reading, she employs literate skills when she needs to, as when she does the family accounts and pays the bills. "She uses literacy but it is not important to her . . . People can get by without revolving their lives around literacy."
- Cliff, divorced and on disability, reads widely. He patronizes the local library, discusses books with his sister, collects Biggles books (a series for boys about a World War II hero), and corresponds with several music-hall entertainers. He also bets the horses, using newspapers, tote books, and racing forms. Cliff uses literacy for pleasure.[36]

35. Brandt (2001); quotation from p. 74.
36. Barton and Hamilton (1999, 128).

As these four portraits suggest, people's private lives display an enormous diversity of reading practices and motivations. Two different kinds of reading emerge, one where reading is the main goal (sit down and read the newspaper) and the other where reading is a means to another end (check out the paper for today's races). People use their repertoire of literacy practices to organize their lives, communicate, entertain themselves, document their experiences, make sense of their worlds, and participate in social life beyond the immediate household. These reading practices are constant, and many are collective as well.

Literary production is cooperative, as a book's Acknowledgements section attests, but the collective nature of readership is less obvious. We tend to envision readers as resembling Jo in *Little Women,* sitting alone by the window reading while munching apples. This "ideology of the solitary reader" ignores the elaborate infrastructure of reading. Reading must be taught, gatekeepers— Oprah Winfrey, the *New York Times Book Review*—steer reading choices, and for many people talking about books is part of the reading experience.[37]

Perhaps the ultimate expression of this form of social literacy is contemporary book clubs (or reading groups), people who meet on a regular basis in their leisure time to discuss books. Elizabeth Long identified 121 such groups active in Houston. Just under two-thirds of these were all women, a mere 3 percent were all men, and the rest were mixed. Focusing on the women's groups, which descend from the nineteenth century women's club movement, Long found that book clubs attract highly educated members who tend to be affluent and somewhat traditional. Most groups grow out of prior circles of acquaintances, but some came from notices put up in bookstores. While many were open to anyone and any book, others had themes—a feminist group, a "Not-So-Great Books" group—or members sharing some characteristic,

37. Becker (1982) describes the "art worlds," networks of coordination and shared conventions from which individual artistic and literary works emerge. The "ideology of the solitary reader" is from Long (2003).

e.g., all Jewish. Members claim the groups satisfied their needs for intellectual stimulation; several groups involved housewives with young children and one comprised women working in technical, male-dominated fields whose members sought intelligent conversation with other women.[38]

Across the Atlantic, Jenny Hartley, who surveyed 350 reading groups in the UK, found the same gender ratio: 69 percent of groups were all female, 4 percent all male (including some of the oldest and most formal groups), and the rest mixed. While reading in groups is not new, the numbers of book clubs mushroomed in the late 1990s. Hartley notes how reading groups do not necessarily compete with but are sometimes facilitated by mass media, especially Oprah's Book Club beginning in 1996 (each month, television personality Oprah Winfrey announced her choice of a book, and a month later devoted half of her show to discussing it). Face-to-face groups in the UK were organized by public libraries, book stores, newspapers, a telecommunications company, *Good Housekeeping,* and entire cities.[39]

Collective reading takes on unusual prominence in myriad "One Book, One City" (or state, or community) programs. The idea originated in 1998 when Nancy Pearl, a librarian and the head of the Washington State Center for the Book, launched a program called "What If All Seattle Read the Same Book?" Although Pearl and her colleagues feared their venture might fall flat, "One Book" programs have proven to be irresistible, for they tap into readers' desires for intelligent discussions, libraries' desires to increase visibility in the community, and mayors' desires to associate their cities with the prestige of literature. "One Book" programs encourage people to read a specific book and organize discussions, readings, performances, and other events pertaining to the book. For example, when Chicago launched its "One Book, One Chicago" program with *To Kill a*

38. Long (2003).

39. Hartley (2001). Note that Internet reading groups are legion, but although both Hartley and Long mention them, they did not include them in their studies.

Mockingbird, the events included a trial reenactment staged by local lawyers downtown at the federal court. Eight years after the Seattle venture, hundreds of "One Book" programs are conducted in every state, and also in Canada, Australia, and the United Kingdom.[40]

Not only mayors promote reading; other politicians and celebrities associate themselves with the virtues of literature and literacy. First Lady Laura Bush, a former librarian, has been unusually active in this regard, promoting the Library of Congress's annual National Book Festival since 2001; reading programs are a favorite of political wives. The First Lady of book promotion would certainly be television celebrity Oprah Winfrey. Oprah's Book Club started in 1996, and although the format has changed over the years—suspending in 2002, restarting with a shift from recent books to classics in 2003, having varying numbers of books annually—the "Oprah effect" on book sales has been unprecedented.[41]

Cities and celebrities sponsor book programs because of the extraordinary value that society places on reading. No other cultural practice gets promoted so aggressively. The unchallenged assumption is that reading and talking about reading contribute to social wellbeing. Educators and librarians and parents, celebrities and politicians, state humanities councils, Centers for the Book, the NEA, the NEH (National Endowment for the Humanities), literary festivals, author tours, talk shows: all celebrate reading books. Regardless of whether or not people are actually spending much time with books, they honor and encourage reading to a remarkable extent.[42]

40. For a list of past and current "One Book" programs, see http://www.loc.gov/loc/cfbook/one-book.html.

41. Economists Butler, Cowan, and Nilsson (2005) show that the impact of an endorsement by Oprah is not only immediate, but long lasting. See also Farr (2005).

42. Some historians (see esp. Graff 1987) have questioned the "literacy myth" that links literacy, schooling, modernization, democracy, and individual social mobility, but such critical voices have had little impact on public thinking.

The social honor accorded to reading is especially noteworthy in light of other media. In 1990 (before the Internet revolution) the Gallup Poll asked how much time respondents had spent "yesterday" using different media. Most people reported spending at least some time listening to the radio, a lot of time watching television, and a little time reading a newspaper, but two-thirds spent no time at all reading magazines or books. As figure 5 shows, there is a fairly wide range of time spent reading books, with about the same percent of people (5–10 percent) spending a half hour, an hour, or two hours with books. Reading for work/school and reading for pleasure occupy about the same amount of time up to two hours; after that, some people (e.g., students) spend four hours or more reading books for work, but almost no one spends that kind of time in leisure reading. The significant point is that 15 percent or so of media users read books for pleasure an hour or more in a typical day. These people—doubtless they are roughly the same people as the 16 percent whom the NEA study counted as "frequent" or "avid" readers—constitute the reading class.[43]

The Gallup Poll has also investigated *why* people use different media. One reason is to relax, and respondents find books and television to be equally relaxing. A second is to do their jobs; over 60 percent of employed respondents see reading speed or comprehension as being very important to their work, so routine reading is essential to many people who are not "readers" in the sense of being deeply engaged with books. A third reason people use media is to learn, and some 60 percent of people think books are the better way to learn. People also report that reading books is "more rewarding" than watching television by a similar 2:1 ratio. Again we see the high esteem that people accord books regardless of whether they actually read many.[44]

43. Gallup Poll (1990; questions 18a–f2). As reported above, the NEA found 46.7% of the population read books at all. This breaks down as 21% light readers (1–5 books per year), 9% moderate readers (6–11 books), 12% frequent readers (12–49 books), and 4% avid readers (50+ books per year). National Endowment for the Arts (2004a, 4).

44. Gallup Poll (2003b). The question on using media for work was, "Think about the skills that you normally use in your job. How important would you say each of the

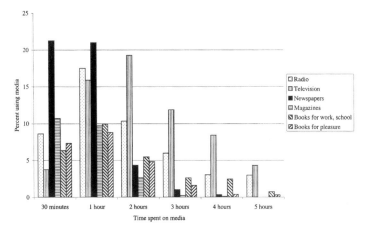

FIGURE 5. Media use previous day, users only

The more people watch TV, the less they read. This inverse relationship has been found constantly since the 1950s, although the magnitude of the difference varies with how the question is asked. Two recent examples: (1) The Roberts and Foehr survey found that older children (11–18) who live in households where the TV is constantly on or who have a TV in their bedrooms spend significantly less time reading, especially reading books, than those without such access; this effect of constantly available television holds regardless of parents' education. (2) The NEA study found readers averaged 2.7 hours of TV per day; non-readers, 3.1 hours.[45]

following skills or subject areas is in doing your job successfully . . . Reading speed or comprehension?" The responses were: Critical, 29.09%; Very important, but not critical, 32.02%; Somewhat important, 25.20%; Not too important, 13.68% (question 23c). When asked "Which of these two activities—watching television or reading books—is . . . the most relaxing?" 46.15% of people chose TV as more relaxing, while 47.7% favored books (question 21a). When asked which is the best way to learn, 59.88 chose books, 30.98% chose TV (question 21b). And when asked which of the two was "the most rewarding," 60.78% picked books, 32.72 picked TV (question 21c).

45. Roberts and Foehr (2004). In an exception to the usual pattern, Ross, McKechnie, and Rothbauer (2006) suggest that people who read also watch more television; this may refer to the gap between media users (including books) and those who do not use any media.

But what about the new media? At the dawn of the Internet age, Sven Birkerts (among others) sounded the death knell of reading:

> Over the past few decades, in the blink on the eye of history, our culture has begun to go through what promises to be a total metamorphosis. The influx of electronic communications and information processing technologies, abetted by the steady improvement of the microprocessor, has rapidly brought on a condition of critical mass. Suddenly it feels like everything is poised for change; the slower world that many of us grew up with dwindles in the rearview mirror. The stable hierarchies of the printed page—one of the defining norms of that world—are being superseded by the rush of impulses through freshly minted circuits. The displacement of the page by the screen is not yet total . . . but the large-scale tendency in that direction has to be obvious to anyone who looks.[46]

Eloquently put, but the situation is actually not so bleak. History suggests that technology and books have been mutually supportive, a symbiosis going well beyond the revolutionary impact of printing. Reading surged when middle-class people became able to afford windows in the eighteenth century. It surged again in the nineteenth century when railroads gave travelers blocks of idle time to fill. The late twentieth century held high hopes, yet unrealized, for e-books. And online libraries will soon bring all the world's libraries to the Internet.[47]

Unlike watching television, going online does not seem to discourage print reading. The NEA study reports that Internet users spent exactly the same amount of time reading as people who never used computers at all. Another review of the research has suggested that the relationship between reading and going

46. Birkerts (1994), 3.

47. For the printing revolution see Eisenstein (1979). The "rise of the novel" thesis, in which windows played a part, is from Watt (1957/1974). Altick (1957) discusses the role train travel played in shaping nineteenth-century reading habits. Already Project Gutenberg makes books that have had their copyright expire available for downloading. Although subject to litigation, the Google Book Search Library Project is making the content of five university libraries available online.

online is not zero-sum but "more-more." Holding education constant—both reading and going online are strongly associated with education—it appears that the heaviest Internet users are also the heaviest readers.[48]

One reason why Internet use might not depress engagement with print media is that, to a significant degree, the Internet actually supports reading. Amazon.com, which started out strictly as a bookseller, was the first e-business that consumers encountered, and it remains a giant in the book trade, as does its online rival Barnesandnoble.com. People tell each other about books in their e-mail and chat rooms. They find out about authors and books on the Internet; a search for "Ernest Hemingway" yields 957,000 hits, "crime novels" fetches 2,500,000, and even Trollope's Palliser series comes up with a respectable 4,780. All of this is a student's dream, but a reader's as well. Recall Cliff, the reader Barton and Hamilton studied who collected Biggles books. If he still does, he probably goes online to pursue his interest: "Biggles books" garners 73,200 hits on Google.[49]

People participate in Internet book groups and they chat in groups devoted to particular authors and genres. Yahoo! supports multiple Anthony Trollope chat groups, for example, with the largest, based on a reading group founded in 1994 that went online in 2000, having 264 active members. The group's home page sets its agenda: "We read Trollope's work in weekly segments and engage in specific discussion of the readings. We also discuss related aspects of Victorian life and culture." And of course people read online constantly, although neither they nor surveys

48. National Endowment for the Arts (2004a), 15. The "more-more" relationship is from Griswold and Wright (2004). Similar findings appear in *IT & Society*'s 2002 collection of articles on "IT, Mass Media, and Other Daily Activity." Although one author (Nie) finds that Internet use depresses reading, the others find either no effect (Robinson, Kestnbaum, Neustadtl, and Alvarez) or a positive effect (Fu, Wang and Qiu; De Haan and Huysmans).

49. All of the searches used Google and were done on February 1, 2005. Of course the "reluctant capitalists" of the book trade have had to respond to online bookselling, both by offering something that online sellers can't (coffee and community) and by going online themselves (Miller 2006).

count this as "reading." Meanwhile, the reverse takes place as well: books and magazines, like *Wired*, devoted to the Internet multiply.[50]

A second reason that going online may not decrease time spent reading is that the "more-more" pattern applies to virtually all forms of cultural participation: some people simply do more than other people do. Richard Peterson has called these folks "cultural omnivores," and they do more of *everything*—attend live performances, listen to music, attend or participate in sports, visit museums—*except* watch television. They also have more catholic tastes, enjoying a wide range of cultural forms. According to a broad review of the research by Ross, McKechnie, and Rothbauer, book readers consume more of every kind of communications media. A "communications elite" consists of the "people who read more books, magazines, and newspapers; go to more films; watch more television [not the usual finding]; and are members of more community associations than the average person." Cultural omnivores, who are typically well educated and middle class, maintain diverse portfolios of cultural capital and have simply added the Internet to their other pursuits.[51]

Other media support reading. The impact of Oprah Winfrey is the supreme case, but books and authors appear on talk shows, on cable channels, on radio interviews, and in other print media. Consider the multiplying effect of something like the *Times Literary Supplement* or the *New York Review of Books*, Garrison Keillor's *Writer's Almanac* or an author interview with Terry Gross on *Fresh Air*. The imagery of dividing up a media pie misses the considerable synergy at work.

50. The Trollope chat group is at http://groups.yahoo.com/group/trollope/. A second group, "Trollope-l: Trollope and His Contemporaries," is somewhat older (online since 1999) and smaller (212 members), but works the same way; it may be found at http://groups.yahoo.com/group/trollope-l/.

51. For the cultural omnivore thesis, see Peterson and Kern (1996). For how omnivores use cultural capital in the workplace, see Erickson (1996). For the relationship between education and wide-ranging tastes, see Bryson 1996. The quotation is from Ross, McKechnie, and Rothbauer (2006, 22–23).

And yet, even omnivores can partake of only so much. At some point the new media, including electronic games, downloaded films, and other high-tech entertainments, must compete with reading for time and attention. As the world becomes ever more wired, what will be the future of reading?[52]

Readers in the Future

In the twenty-first century reading seems to be both honored and abandoned. Is it possible to reconcile the evidence that Internet use does not depress reading with the evidence that reading is declining overall? How can the proliferation of reading groups, Trollope websites, book superstores, festivals of the book, and the Oprah effect be part of the same universe as the NEA report's plummeting percentages of readers, as well university undergraduate libraries that are entirely free of books? How can books be both ignored and sacred?[53]

The answer lies in the emergence—or, historically speaking, the re-emergence—of a reading class. An elite segment of the general population, one that is highly educated, affluent, metropolitan, and young, has produced both heavy readers and early adopters of the Internet. Exhibiting the concentration effect, they read more than the average readers of the past. Right now these people—the avid readers, the communications elite, the cultural

52. The NEA study, although it did not directly ask if people substituted Internet surfing for reading, notes that the major drop in literary reading occurred in the 1990s, the same time when large numbers of people started going online.

53. The *New York Times* reported on May 14, 2005, that the University of Texas had announced that by summer its undergraduate library would consist of "a 24-hour electronic information commons," with all the books dispersed to other collections (Blumenthal 2005). The situation is not quite as dire as the secondary headline suggests. Academic librarians, who generally support such changes, point out that universities created undergraduate libraries at a time when their graduate research libraries were restricted to faculty and graduate students; these restrictions have largely vanished, leaving the undergraduate libraries as "increasingly puny adjuncts with duplicate collections and shelves of light reading." But symbolically this move by a major research university is significant, and as one Texas student protested, "Well, this is a library—it's supposed to have books in it."

omnivores, much of "the creative class"—along with older, less technologically advanced, long-committed readers, make up the reading class.[54]

As Internet use moves to older groups (both because of late adoption by older people and by the aging of early users) and into less advantaged segments of the population, the more-more pattern may not move with it. For the less advantaged groups, whose leisure time is more limited and whose reading habits are less firmly established, reading will have little appeal. The competition from electronic media will soak up whatever leisure time might have gone into reading; television and electronic games have paved the way here.

Reading for entertainment by the general population is something very rare and very recent. Reading has always been associated with education and with urban social elites. Although contemporary commentators deplore the decline of "the reading habit" or "literary reading," historically the era of mass reading, which lasted from the mid-nineteenth through the mid-twentieth century in northwestern Europe, Japan, and North America, was the anomaly. Today reading is returning to its former, narrower social base: a self-perpetuating minority that I have called the reading class.[55]

While nineteenth- and twentieth-century stratification involved *what* people read (e.g., the classical canon versus working-class newspapers or confession magazines), the new century may resemble earlier eras when a fundamental social divide involved *whether* people read. Unlike in the past, virtually everyone in the developed world and a majority in poorer countries will be capable of reading, and most will read as part of their jobs,

54. Although there is overlap between the reading class and the "creative class" defined by Florida (2002), in part because they are both highly educated, the two groups are not congruent. Some groups Florida includes (software engineers, business managers) may not be heavy readers, while librarians and high school teachers, reading-class stalwarts, are not included in Florida's group of highly mobile creative professionals.

55. For the nineteenth-century emergence of popular reading in England, see Altick (1957), Watt (1957), and Rose (2001). For Japan, see Huffman 1997. For Sweden, see Johansson (1977).

online activities, and everyday business of living. Only a minority, however, will read books for pleasure on a regular basis. Books are already less omnipresent in people's lives than other media are, and this will continue. Many of the educated will still be voracious readers, and—critically—reading will retain and even increase its prestige as it becomes seen as an endangered practice. Institutions will celebrate and facilitate reading. Non-readers will honor it and encourage it among their children. Reading will not just give access to cultural capital: the practice itself will *be* cultural capital.

An educated, metropolitan elite will read extensively and intensively. Society—schools, governments, the market, the Internet, other media, and the culture at large—will support and honor its practice. Monuments, street names, national holidays, and plaques on houses pointed out by tour guides will continue to lend everyday support to the prestige of books, writers, and reading. The never ending avalanche of books by politicians and celebrities will attest to the prestige that print carries. For reading is not just a peculiar form of entertainment for those who can afford it, like playing polo, but a way for powerful people to communicate with one another. This shows no sign of diminishing.[56]

History and contemporary practices make three things clear, and these three things define the future of reading. First is reading's sheer, enduring prestige. Among the Lancaster residents they studied, Barton and Hamilton found that the idea of being "a reader" is imbued with values. Reading is seen as a good thing, and people equate reading with being bright. Earlier British working-class attitudes that had disparaged readers as lazy or

---

56. Garrison Keillor's *Writer's Almanac* (American Public Media), February 2, 2005, points out that "On June 16, 1924, the twentieth anniversary of Bloomsday, Joyce wrote in his notebook, 'Twenty years after. Will anyone remember this date?' Today, June 16th is a holiday in Ireland that rivals St. Patrick's Day. It's one of the only national holidays in the world that's based not on anyone's birthday or on a religious or a historical event, but merely upon a date in a work of fiction." For street names and monuments see Ferguson (1987).

antisocial have faded. This prestige has provoked critique, for literacy is strongly associated with social inequality, but this has had virtually no impact on the social honor accorded to reading and to "being a reader."[57]

Second, reading is a product of social organization, and an immense infrastructure supports it. Educational institutions, media tie-ins, non-profits, and entire industries encourage and sustain reading. Consider just the reading-group phenomenon. The United States (and to a lesser extent other book club countries like the UK, Australia, and New Zealand) has paid group leaders, book-club consultants, coordinators, books on how to organize a book club, reading-group questions in the back of paperback editions—all in all a considerable "book club service industry." We might call this the pile-on effect: reading practices, once they reach some critical mass, generate their own support structure.[58]

The third element that will shape reading in the future, a consequence of the first two, is the increasing division between reading as a matter-of-fact practice of just about everyone, and reading—the reading of literature, of serious nonfiction, of the quality press—as an esteemed, cultivated, supported practice of an educated elite. The gap between these two seems likely to widen. The reading class, influential and enabled, will flourish even as reading by the general public will continue to decline.

This reading class is culturally powerful and it is critical to the perpetuation of regionalism. Members of the reading class define the conceptual categories that orient people's lives. In what many regard as the post-print culture of the contemporary world, readers produce and reproduce regionalism. They celebrate local authors, they read regional mysteries, they support independent bookstores with strong community ties. The same pile-on infrastructure that supports reading in general supports regionalism in particular.

57. For the fading of working-class suspicion, see Barton and Hamilton (1998, 158). For a critical view, see Stuckey (1991).

58. For a discussion of the infrastructure supporting reading groups see Hartley (2001), esp. 118 See also Long (2003).

But not always, and not always in the same way. Context (the literary system of production and distribution; the political and economic and demographic configurations) and culture (the meanings and implications entailed in a place's particular expressions of the regionalist aesthetic) enable some reader-regionalism links and block others. The following case studies show when and how literary regionalism emerges.

3

Cowbirds in America

WITH NATHAN WRIGHT[1]

Regional literature does not simply sprout from its native soil. If it ever constituted some authentic and inevitable cultural expression of people bound to and shaped by the land, such an ideal type is no longer the case (it probably never was). Today regional literature both depends upon state and institutional support and upon the market. Most of all, it requires a reading class that is interested in reading about place.

To explore this relationship between the reading class and regional literature, we begin with the United States. Does regional culture still exist in America? Can it withstand both the movement of people and the pressures toward homogenized sights, sounds, tastes, and experiences? If regional culture endures in a dynamic social context, what processes maintain or recreate it?

To gain some empirical purchase on these broad questions requires research on specific forms of regional culture and specific aspects of contemporary social dynamics. This chapter looks at the relationship between regional literary culture on the one

1. This chapter is a shortened version of Griswold and Wright (2004).

hand and residential mobility on the other. Regional literature is just one form of place-based cultural expression, of course; regional food, dialect, and music are others, and they affect more people. Literature impacts the culturally powerful reading class, however, thereby magnifying its influence. Similarly, residential mobility is just one element of the dynamics characteristic of postmodern, global societies. But it is a significant element, and it is not disappearing. In the last half of the twentieth century, American residential mobility—specifically the percent of natives born in states other than their current state of residence—steadily increased. Therefore, regional literature offers insight into the more general social dynamics that might threaten regional cultures.[2]

Drawing on an extraordinary Internet survey sponsored by the National Geographic Society, this chapter explores the relationship between mobility and regionalism. It shows that literary regionalism is persisting, and that mobility itself is helping to reproduce it through the "cowbirds" who move into a region and catch up with those born there in terms of their local cultural knowledge. The conclusion argues that a dynamic social context, far from chipping away at enduring regionalism, actually produces it.

Karl Marx famously noted that time was annihilating space in the modern era. In his 1857–58 notebooks (not published until 1941 as the *Grundrisse* [sketches]), Marx argued that that, "While capital . . . must strive to tear down every barrier . . . to exchange and conquer the whole earth for its markets, it strives on the other side to annihilate this space with time." He seemed to have two ideas in mind: distances no longer mattered, given the

2. In 1950, 68% of the total population was born in the state of their current residence; this figure dropped to 67% in 1960, 65% in 1970, 64% in 1980, and 62% in 1990. The difference is not due to an increase in the foreign-born population, which went down (from 6.9% in 1950 to 4.8% in 1970) and then up (to 7.9% in 1990). The native population's mobility steadily increased as well; in 1950, 27% lived in a state other than their birth state, and this figure rose to 33% in 1990. U.S. Census Bureau, *Statistical Abstract of the United States: 2000*. Table 46: Native and Foreign-Born Populations by Place of Birth: 1950–1990.

technological advances in communication and transportation, and industrial capitalism had reduced places to the same cash nexus as everything else.[3]

As was seen in the first chapter, many observers have followed a similar logic to the conclusion that technology and globalization are rendering geography irrelevant, leaving people with "no sense of place." Late modernity has brought a transition from local culture to global culture. In the "before" condition (before the flows of goods, information, finance, and labor washed over the globe), culture expressed the social and economic experience of a particular place. Jurisdictional boundaries—especially those of the state—and clearly demarcated markets ratified and hemmed in such situated cultures, just as the placement of the body constrained human action. In the "after" condition, markets are global, state boundaries are porous, people are virtual as well as frequent flyers, and cultures soar about on electronic wings, mixing and mingling in cyberspace. Such a global culture would seem to threaten, if not eclipse, people's sense of place.[4]

3. Marx (1993, 539).

4. *No Sense of Place* was the title of one the most influential statements of the decline of place (Meyrowitz 1985) discussed in chap. 1, this volume. See also Haraway (1990) for a vivid portrait of disembodied "cyborgs." "Place" made something of a comeback in the century's last decade, however, with the dawning recognition of how postmodernity and globalization make possible new spatial arrangements and meanings. For a leading exemplar of more current thinking, see Harvey (1990, 1993). Harvey represents the encounter between Marxian and postmodernist theory in his analyses of the political economy of place—e.g., global capital's mobility in terms of both production and consumption; the construction of new places to absorb excess capital—and the apparent human need for spatial grounding that prompts the construction of "place." Responding to Harvey and other theorists of capitalism and space, Doreen Massey (1984, 1993) has pointed to a "power geometry" in which different groups—especially men versus women—are situated differently with respect to capitalism's various flows of labor and finance. (For other discussions of the relationship between space and gender, see also Spain (1992) and Hochschild (1997). For globalization theories, see Bhabha (1994), esp. ch. 6, where Bhabha points out how print was both agent and symptom of this separating process.) Optimists see these new formations as creating a flexible and cosmopolitan localism with the capacity for "empathetic sociality" (Maffesoli 1996), while pessimists point out that the new, globally supported localism can be as divisive as the old provincialism (Lash and Urry 1994, esp. ch. 11; Castells 1989; Glaeser 2000).

What happens when the forces of global culture come bearing down on local cultures? If the local is not obliterated, is it transformed? How, and how consistently? Years ago Raymond Williams distinguished among four types of culture: dominant, oppositional, residual, and emergent. Localism, once dominant, would appear to be the residual type that perhaps becomes the alternative to mass media domination (as Williams, himself a provincial, would have anticipated). But could new forms of localism be, in fact, emergent?[5]

The persistence of regionalism, this chapter will show, is not simply residual, something which has successfully defied change. Instead, it is in large part emergent, for the very movement of people and of cultural objects helps produce this persistence of local cultural patterns. In other words, regional culture, like other forms of localism, is not opposed to, but actually is characteristic of global culture.

The Culture of Place in a Restless World

The cultural complexity of today's world involves the movement of ideas, images, goods, money, and people. This chapter looks at the last of these, focusing specifically on residential mobility. It tries to establish whether local cultures persist and asks whether or not mobility affects people's knowledge of their local culture.

The cultural object of analysis is regional literature. The adjective "regional," defined as "of or relating to a region of a country," may be attached to a work of literature or to an author. In this chapter, regional literature is defined by author: regional literature is the writing of authors who are strongly associated with particular places. Many of America's most prominent writers— Faulkner, Cather, Steinbeck, Thoreau—have been regionalists in this sense. Regional authors do not always write about their regions (though they often do), but nevertheless their regions claim them.

5. Williams (1977).

Do such claims matter? Regional practices in the consumption of literature offer a good case through which to examine the question of whether cultural localism is or is not disappearing. Print culture has always been associated with breaking down provincialism. More recently, book sales via Amazon.com served as an advance guard for e-commerce. And the reading class is generally educated and cosmopolitan. So if neither the supply of nor the demand for literature is constrained by geography, the presence of a geographic influence on literary knowledge and tastes would seem to indicate some persistent or emergent cultural regionalism.

Asking questions about the current state of literary regionalism, and about the reading practices of people who move around versus people who stay in place, allows us to examine some of the processes whereby the global and the local, the cosmopolitan and the provincial, interact. First, is there a recognized regional literary culture? Specifically, do people know about and read the writers from the region in which they live, or is there "no sense of place" in people's literary preferences? Second, what is the relationship between geographic mobility and cultural participation, here measured by familiarity with a wide variety of canonical and popular authors? And third, what is the relationship between geographic mobility and literary regionalism, measured by familiarity with authors associated with the region of the reader's current residence?

Answers to these three questions suggest patterns of regional cultural engagement that may be emerging in a highly mobile society. They illuminate both the cultural participation of mobile people and the fate of regional literary culture in general, particularly given what Anthony Giddens calls the "distanciation" between cultural forms of identification and geographical place that many see as characteristic of late modernity. An unusual survey allowed us to explore these questions in some detail.[6]

6. See Giddens (1990).

Survey2000

Our data come from Survey2000, an online survey conducted by the National Geographic Society. The data analyzed here consisted of those 22,579 respondents who (1) are currently living in the U.S. and (2) completed the literature module in its entirety. These people—Internet users, comfortable with answering questions about literature—are largely members of the reading class.[7]

One of the purposes of Survey2000 was to examine the differences between people who move around a lot and those who stay in place. Respondents were asked where they lived at birth and at seven-year intervals up to and including their current residence. The present chapter defines "movers" versus "stayers" by comparing respondents' region of current residence with region of birth; for movers, the two were different, while for stayers, they were the same.[8]

Survey2000 asked a set of questions about regional culture, involving food, music, and literature. Respondents to the literature module were presented with the names of twenty-eight authors. Up to four of these were authors from or strongly associated with the state of the respondent's birth, four from where they lived at the age of fourteen, four at their residence at twenty-one, four from the state of current residence, and four from some random

7. Sociologist James Witte was the principal investigator. Of the 40,620 adults from the U.S. who started the survey, 81% completed the base survey and at least one randomly assigned cultural module (on literature, music, or food), even though doing so typically took them an hour or more. Thus the survey, which was online for two months in fall 1998, has an unusually high number of respondents. For a fuller discussion of the mechanics of this particular survey and the justification for online surveys in general, see Witte, Amoroso, and Howard (2000); Witte and Howard (2002); and Witte (2003). For methodological issues involving the representativeness of the survey, see Griswold and Wright (2004).

8. The National Geographic Society had in mind comparing the community attachments of the two groups, and a number of cultural sociologists were interested in seeing if and how mobility affected people's cultural participation. Community attachment was examined by Barry Wellman and Keith Hampton and by James Witte. Cultural participation was studied by William S. Bainbridge, Bonnie Erickson, Richard A. Peterson, and Bethany Bryson, as well as by the authors of this chapter.

other state in which the respondent had lived. In addition to these, respondents saw four names from a list of "General Authors," writers who are well known but not strongly associated with any one state, and the rest randomly drawn from the entire list of authors. For each author respondents indicated whether they had ever heard of the author, whether they had read anything by that author, or whether they recommended that author to others. The mean of these cumulated answers, which respondents indicated on a 0–3 scale, constituted the recognition score for each author. Appendix A lists the general authors and the authors associated with each state in each census region.[9]

9. Each respondent was presented one of the three culture modules—food, music, or literature. After answering those questions, they were asked if they wanted to go on to the other modules. Of the 40,420 respondents who started the survey, 80.6% completed the entire base survey plus at least one of the culture modules, and 49.6% completed all three of the culture modules. There were 22,579 respondents who completed the base survey plus the entire literature module. These respondents make up our sample, though we further limited them to those with at least a bachelor's degree.

The procedure of selecting four authors from five states associated with five different points in the life course could yield a total of twenty different names. Usually it produced fewer than twenty names, however, for two reasons: First, not all states had four or more authors associated with the state. If a state had more than four authors, the four were selected randomly; if the state had four or fewer, each was used. The list of authors appears in appendix A. The second reason that fewer than twenty names might have been generated is that generating the maximum number of names would mean: (1) that the respondent was over twenty-one, and (2) that he or she lived in at least five different states, one at birth, one at fourteen, one at twenty-one, one currently, and a fifth at some other point in his or her life. The first of these conditions was not always the case, and the second one rarely was.

We used multiple methods to identify authors "strongly identified" with a state: consultation with various literature professors; perusal of the courses on regional literature offered at state universities; bookstores; anthologies and reference sources, including *The Oxford Companion to American Literature, The Oxford Illustrated Literary Guide to the United States,* the *Encyclopedia of Frontier and Western Fiction,* and the *Encyclopedia of Southern Culture.* We used both general anthologies, such as *The Local Colorists: American Short Stories, 1957–1900* and the *Norton Anthology of Literature by Women,* and also regional and state anthologies, like *Downhome: An Anthology of Southern Women Writers; The Last Best Place: A Montana Anthology;* and *Maine Speaks: An Anthology of Maine Writers.* We consulted websites of the state humanities councils to see which writers were featured. And we asked people from the state. Opportunism helped: for example when Griswold found herself standing in an airport line behind a couple from Boise, she asked them, "Pardon me, but can you tell me who are Idaho's best-known

FIGURE 6. Map of most-recognized authors by nine census regions

The Persistence of Place

Given the familiar pressures toward homogenization, even globalization, of culture, do readers have a "sense of place" that influences their literary knowledge and preferences? Given our belief
that a relationship between culture and place is not disappearing
under the impact of globalization or world culture, we hypoth-
esized that we would indeed find evidence of substantial literary
regionalism. Using the nine census regions indicated on the map
comprising figure 6, we looked to see which authors were among
the thirty most widely recognized within each region. Appendix

writers?" and they each replied, without hesitation, "You mean aside from Ernest Hemingway?"

Hemingway exemplifies another characteristic of "strong association," which is that
several states often "claim" the same writer. Using the methods just described, we find
that Hemingway is an Illinois writer, a Florida writer, an Idaho writer—and even a
Michigan writer. Zane Grey is claimed by several western states, though for the purposes of Survey2000 he was a Utah writer, and there are other similar cases. The nature
of the analysis required us to assign a writer to a single state; Hemingway is an Idaho
writer, not an Illinois writer in Survey2000. This does not mean that Idaho's claim is
somehow more valid, but it does mean that Idaho respondents were more likely to see
his name. Hemingway and Grey are probably the most worrisome cases of assigning a
writer with broad appeal to one particular state. Nevertheless, they are indeed strongly
associated with their respective states, especially by the people who live in these states,
as the airport incident illustrates.

B shows the authors most recognized by all respondents and by the respondents currently residing in each region.[10]

While there are plenty of writers whose appeal is nationwide, figure 6 and appendix B both suggest that readers favor writers from or associated with their own regions. Some writers appeal chiefly in the East, like F. Scott Fitzgerald, while others, like James Michener, are primarily Western writers. In New England, the number two author is Robert Frost, while in the Pacific region, number two is John Steinbeck. No doubt schools play a role here, with Steinbeck appearing on more required-reading lists in California than in New Hampshire. Education isn't everything, however, for as the case of Michener suggests, one finds regionalism at play with popular authors as well as canonical ones. Stephen King and John Grisham are two hugely popular writers who would be unlikely to appear on any high school curriculum and who might be supposed to transcend any regional appeal. Notice, though, that Grisham doesn't even make the top ten in New England, while he is several notches ahead of King in East South Central.

Individual authors exhibit a surprising degree of regional appeal. Consider the case of Garrison Keillor, an author-entertainer who is well known nationally through public radio broadcasting, yet who is a regionalist in terms of the content of both his writing and his *Prairie Home Companion* program. The states indicated in figure 7 gave him recognition scores of 1.6 or higher. This is Garrison Keillor country. Like Stephen King, Keillor is more locally specific in his appeal than one might have guessed.

The descriptive data so far suggest that readers do indeed have a "sense of place" in that they tend to favor authors from their own part of the country. The answer to the first of our three questions—do people favor writers from their own regions?—is clear: yes, they do. Is this a case of old timers holding on, maintaining

10. For these comparisons we are excluding Alaska and Hawaii. Hawaii produced flawed data because of a programming error. The Alaska data is sound and may be included in later analyses, but the relatively small N and the fact that it is the only case where a state and region are the same made us decide not to include it here.

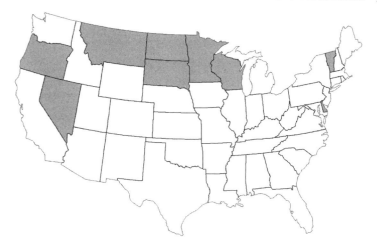

FIGURE 7. States with high recognition scores for Garrison Keillor

their cultural roots? To answer this we need to assess the relationship between mobility and regionalism. We want to look at the effects of mobility, the effects of regional variation, and the interactions between the two.

For purposes of quantitative analyses, the following dependent variables were constructed, three indicating overall knowledge of literature with the fourth one indicating knowledge of literature particular to a region:

- *Average score for top 20 authors.* All 252 authors viewed were ranked according to their overall mean recognition score (on a scale of 0–3) among all respondents who viewed them. The top 20 of these we imagine to be the most well known authors to respondents to this survey. This variable is the mean score for those authors each respondent viewed that comprise these top 20 authors.
- *Average score for all authors respondent viewed.* Each respondent viewed 28 authors, some associated with states they lived in at various points in their life and the rest from the list of 31 "General" authors not seen as regionally focused and randomly assigned from the total list of 252 authors (see details in note 9). This variable is the mean score for all 28 authors viewed by each respondent.

- *Average score for all general authors.* Each respondent was randomly assigned some authors from a list of 31 "General" authors who are generally well known but not typically linked to any one state. This variable is the mean score for those of the 31 general authors that were actually viewed by each respondent.
- *Average score for all authors from respondent's region.* Each respondent saw a number of authors from the region in which he or she currently lives. This variable is the mean score for those authors viewed who come from the respondent's current region of residence.

We will consider first the more general issue raised in our second question, the relationship between mobility and familiarity with literature. The hypothesis, following both globalization theory and the older distinction between "provincials" versus "cosmopolitans," was that movers would be more culturally knowledgeable than stayers.

Table 1 shows some descriptive data comparing the author-recognition scores of stayers and movers. (Note that the data here represent bivariate relationships that do not control for other factors; multivariate analyses will follow.) It suggests that there is something to the provincials/cosmopolitans distinction: people who move around know more about literature than people who do not. This is the case whether we are talking about the twenty

TABLE 1   General knowledge of authors, movers vs. stayers

	Mobility	
Authors	Stayers	Movers
Top 20 authors	1.9869	2.0307
	(.5872)	(.6525)
All 28 authors viewed	.6112	.6440
	(.3299)	(.3289)
31 general authors	1.0048	1.0439
	(.5246)	(.5326)

Note: Respondents are Survey2000 participants with a bachelor's degree or more education. The numbers in parentheses are standard deviations.

most popular authors, the authors actually viewed, or those authors considered "general authors" who are not tightly linked to any one region. Table 1 shows that if we look at those respondents who have a bachelor's degree or above, for example, we see that movers have slightly higher average scores than stayers in all three categories. So it appears that movers know more about literature than stayers do, but these differences are slight (though statistically significant) and may not hold up when multivariate analyses are done.[11]

Despite what appears to be movers' greater literary knowledge overall, common sense suggests that stayers would know more about their regional culture than movers do. If movers have more literary knowledge than stayers, however, could it be that cultural regionalism is not related to stability versus mobility? Assessing this counterintuitive possibility requires a more refined analysis, one that takes into account both the main effects of mobility and living in different regions and the interaction effects of moving into each specific region. In order to do this, additional dependent variables were used to measure knowledge of literature particular to each region.

Table 2 presents Eta-squared results for one-way analyses of variance (ANOVA) of the three overall literary knowledge dependent variables—knowledge of top twenty authors, of all authors seen, and of authors from the general authors list—and the average score for all authors from respondent's current region of residence. Results indicate proportion of explained variation

---

11. We broke respondents into four educational categories: high school diploma or lower, some college but no bachelor's degree, bachelor's degree only, or higher than bachelor's degree. For each, we looked at the scores given to the top twenty authors, the twenty-eight authors actually viewed, and the general authors. In all twelve cases, the movers scored higher than the stayers.

As explained earlier, Survey2000 is not a random sample and thus we are technically unable to quantify statistical significance because we cannot rely on the claims of the central limit theorem. Nevertheless, we conducted traditional tests of statistical significance and present them at $p < .001$ level because we think many of our readers would like to know which of our differences meet these standards and which do not. As with all matters statistical, however, we ask our readers to pay attention to the substantive differences in our findings without making too much of statistical significance.

TABLE 2 Eta-squared results for one-way ANOVAS

	Average score for top 20 authors	Average score for all authors respondent viewed	Average score for all general authors	Average score for all authors from respondent's region
Movers vs. stayers	.001*	.002*	.001*	.002*
Bachelor's vs. graduate degree	.009*	.018*	.009*	.010*
Knowledge of literature	.074*	.152*	.116*	.059*
Sex	.014*	.029*	.047*	.009*
Region of residence	.004*	.006*	.005*	.042*

Note: Respondents are Survey2000 participants with a bachelor's degree or more education.
* $P < .001$

in the dependent variable explained by key independent variables (without controlling for the other independent variables).

The table shows what we would expect for the three overall literary-knowledge measures: respondents' education, self-reported literary knowledge, and gender each explain substantive amounts of variation. As table 1 suggested, movers may know slightly more about literature overall than stayers, although the amount of explained variation is trivial. Similarly, there are some regional differences in overall knowledge of literature, but again the amount of explained variation is trivial.[12]

Before turning to the right-hand column of table 2, we should look at the mover/stayer issue more closely. We have seen that movers know a bit more about literature than stayers do. At every

12. The Eta-squared for education is small because these analyses are limited to those respondents with a bachelor's degree or higher. Thus they test the difference between those with a bachelor's degree and those with a graduate degree. When all respondents are included, education explains roughly 4.5 percent of the variation in the three measures of overall literary knowledge, and less than 3 percent of the variation in recognition of one's own region's authors.

educational level, people who live in a different region from that of their birth know more authors than people who live in the region they were born in; this is the cosmopolitan effect. Common sense suggests, however, that this would not be true in the case of regional authors. It seems more likely that people who have stayed in some place are more deeply steeped in its local culture than people who have arrived more recently.

This deep-roots theory, believed by just about everyone, may be mistaken. Survey2000 stayers do indeed know more about authors from their *birth* regions than do movers, but the difference for knowledge about authors from their *current* region all but disappears. And if we look at the level of state rather than region, movers seem largely to catch up with stayers.[13]

Table 3 demonstrates that stayers know almost as much about authors from the state they were born in or lived in at early ages as they do about authors from their current state. This is hardly surprising, for they may be still living in the same state as their birth state (for stayers, the birth state is within the same region as the state in which they currently live, but it may or may not be the same state). For movers, on the other hand, the birth state is (by definition) located in a different region from their state of current residence. While movers know considerably less about the literary culture of the state in which they were born than stayers do (.6645 vs. .7586), the knowledge gap narrows if we look at the state in which they now live (.7461 vs. .7832). In other words, movers are not much different than stayers, despite their lack of local roots.

Turning again to table 2, we see that the ANOVA results for regional literary knowledge are different from the results for the three overall literary knowledge variables. Though education,

13. Movers had a recognition score of .6020 of authors from their birth region, while stayers had a score of .6342. The difference narrows when we look at recognition scores for current region, which is .6249 for movers, only slightly lower than the .6342 for the stayers. This fails to control for the overall popularity of each author seen by each respondent, however, and thus cannot be seen as definitive. We correct for this in the multivariate analyses below.

TABLE 3   Mean state author recognition scores for
stayers and movers

| | Mobility | |
Respondent's age	Stayers	Movers
Birth	.7586	.6645
	(.6290)	(.6691)
Age 14	.7730	.7134
	(.6800)	(.6464)
Age 21	.7529	.7168
	(.6761)	(.6512)
Current	.7832	.7461
	(.6817)	(.6971)

Note: Respondents are Survey2000 participants with a
bachelor's degree or more education. The four time points
under age indicate when the respondent lived in the state he or
she claimed. Numbers in parentheses are standard deviations.

self-reported literary knowledge, and sex still explain substantive
amounts of the variation in respondents' recognition of authors
from their region of current residence, these variables are not as
important as they were in explaining variation in recognition of
authors overall. In contrast, the region in which a respondent
currently lives explains over 4 percent of the variation in recognition of authors from the respondent's region. This indicates that
though regional differences account for very little in explaining
overall knowledge of literature, regional differences are very important in explaining knowledge of regional literature. Note also
that the differences between movers and stayers remain trivial
when it comes to explaining variation in recognition of one's own
regional authors. This also suggests that the deep-roots theory
may be mistaken.

Yet not all regions are likely to be the same in terms of recognizing their own authors and in terms of movers catching up
to stayers. Table 4 gives the mean recognition scores for each region's set of authors (and for all twenty-eight authors viewed by

TABLE 4 Mean recognition scores for all authors

Respondent	Author										All 28 authors viewed
	New England	Middle Atlantic	East North Central	West North Central	South Atlantic	East South Central	West South Central	Mountain	Pacific	Alaska	
New England	**.9392** (**.5905**)	.5657 (.6616)	.5335 (.6603)	.7349 (.8911)	.4897 (.6362)	.6152 (.8224)	.5365 (.6905)	.4313 (.6238)	.5195 (.7427)	.1227 (.3782)	.6941 (.3461)
Middle Atlantic	.6339 (.7272)	**.5818** (**.5366**)	.5399 (.6838)	.7212 (.8395)	.4716 (.5930)	.5892 (.8129)	.5014 (.6891)	.3968 (.5802)	.5253 (.7327)	.1005 (.3147)	.6032 (.3277)
East North Central	.6209 (.7446)	.4724 (.6517)	**.6006** (**.5299**)	.7205 (.8412)	.4272 (.5731)	.5956 (.8009)	.4795 (.6673)	.3896 (.6003)	.4973 (.7195)	.0947 (.3152)	.5888 (.3248)
West North Central	.6264 (.7367)	.4779 (.6991)	.4798 (.6068)	**1.0311** (**.7002**)	.4283 (.5755)	.6046 (.7487)	.5563 (.7211)	.4312 (.6231)	.4896 (.6811)	.1024 (.3294)	.6187 (.3167)
South Atlantic	.6278 (.7301)	.5490 (.6748)	.4989 (.6289)	.7028 (.8330)	**.6360** (**.5529**)	.6086 (.8042)	.5462 (.7218)	.4099 (.6232)	.5455 (.7336)	.1113 (.3664)	.6300 (.3256)
East South Central	.6176 (.7219)	.5810 (.7061)	.4821 (.6004)	.6842 (.8218)	.5534 (.6076)	**.6154** (**.7063**)	.5762 (.7537)	.4195 (.5804)	.4815 (.6611)	.0854 (.3221)	.6111 (.3541)
West South Central	.6301 (.7237)	.5463 (.7297)	.4868 (.6441)	.6877 (.8053)	.4547 (.6179)	.6381 (.8259)	**.7437** (**.5625**)	.3891 (.6001)	.5458 (.7458)	.0858 (.3037)	.6152 (.3412)
Mountain	.6594 (.7827)	.5369 (.6983)	.4949 (.6215)	.8013 (.8823)	.4407 (.5951)	.6134 (.8118)	.5760 (.7000)	**.6709** (**.5689**)	.5706 (.7173)	.0922 (.2841)	.6362 (.3388)
Pacific	.6274 (.7274)	.5216 (.6811)	.5030 (.6381)	.7777 (.8877)	.4819 (.6098)	.5849 (.7918)	.5560 (.7099)	.4737 (.6315)	**.7127** (**.6186**)	.0912 (.3244)	.6362 (.3308)
Alaska	.6000 (.7010)	.5810 (.7098)	.4264 (.5768)	.8366 (.9145)	.5401 (.6520)	.5500 (.7825)	.5798 (.8289)	.5789 (.7003)	.5401 (.6277)	**.6839** (**.8460**)	.6596 (.3243)
Overall	*.6530* (*.7293*)	*.5360* (*.6642*)	*.5189* (*.6218*)	*.7566* (*.8458*)	*.5036* (*.5945*)	*.6030* (*.7963*)	*.5624* (*.6944*)	*.4457* (*.6140*)	*.5720* (*.7037*)	*.1283* (*.3937*)	*.6245* (*.3321*)

Note: Respondents are Survey2000 participants with a bachelor's degree or more education. Numbers in parentheses are standard deviations. Boldface numbers are those critical to the text's discussion.

each respondent) broken down by respondents living in each region. It seems to indicate four general patterns: (1) respondents living in a region seem to recognize their own authors more than respondents living outside the region; (2) some regions seem to recognize their own authors better than others; (3) some regions' authors are better known across the country than others are; and (4) some regions seem to know more about all literature than do others.

By itself, this table is incomplete and misleading in two ways. It fails to control for other factors and it fails to address the questions of mobility. For these reasons, multivariate regressions were done for each region's set of authors. The following independent variables are used as predictors of author recognition:

- *Popularity control.* Since each respondent saw a different set of authors, the popularity control averages together the mean scores for each author presented to the respondent that were given to each author by all respondents overall. For instance, if respondent "Jane" saw six authors from New England, the overall mean recognition scores for each of those 6 authors (as scored by all respondents who viewed them) are averaged together to create this control. This control functions as an expected familiarity level that each respondent should have with his or her set of authors viewed. Thus, the effects noted for the other independent variables are net of the overall popularity of each author from each region.
- *Sex.* This is dummy coded, with males as the omitted category.
- *Age.* This is measured in absolute number of years lived.
- *Education.* Since we limited our analyses to the college educated, this is a dummy variable for having a graduate degree, with those holding only a bachelor's degree as the omitted category.[14]
- *Average score for all general authors.* This is used as a proxy for respondent's general knowledge of literature, not specific to region.[15]

14. All regressions were also done without limiting respondents to those with a bachelor's degree. This led to education explaining much more variation in recognition of regional authors, but did not substantively change any of the other findings at all.

15. This measure does not overlap at all with the regional authors because authors were either assigned to a particular state or to the list of general authors, never to both.

- *Netters.* A dichotomous variable was created indicating persons who had used the Internet regularly for longer than two years at the time of taking the survey. Using the Internet for longer than two years prior to the time the survey was online would indicate that they were regularly using the Internet at a time when Internet-service providers were not widely available in one's home. Thus, these respondents are considered to be early adopters of the Internet and likely to be knowledgeable and heavy Internet users. This variable is dummy coded with those who did not use the Internet for longer than two years prior to the survey as the omitted category.
- *Movers.* A dichotomous variable was created indicating respondents who at the time of the survey reported living in a region other than the region of their birth. These movers are opposed to stayers, who reported currently living in the same region as the region of their birth. This variable is dummy coded with stayers as the omitted category.
- *Region of current residence.* This multichotomous variable refers to the region in which respondents reported that they were currently residing. It is zero-effect coded with Alaska as the omitted category. The zero-effect coding of this variable means that coefficients refer to differences relative to the mean of the means of all regions, not differences relative to Alaska.
- *Moving into region.* This is an interaction term for being a mover and living in the particular region of interest.

These regressions allow us to answer several important questions. Does region matter in terms of recognizing authors? If so, how? And what is the role of mobility? We hypothesize that respondents living in the region will recognize their own authors more than those living in other regions (the "regionalism" hypothesis). With regard to mobility, we can specify a few different hypotheses to be tested by these regressions. First, we hypothesize a cosmopolitan effect of moving in general. We suspect that movers will know more about authors in general, regardless of where they've moved from or where they've moved to, and

---

All regressions were also done using respondent's self-reported knowledge of literature and this did not alter any of the substantive findings at all.

TABLE 5 Unstandardized regression coefficients for recognition scores for all authors associated with each region where respondent lives currently

	New England	Middle Atlantic	East North Central	West North Central	South Atlantic	East South Central	West South Central	Mountain	Pacific	Alaska	All 28 authors viewed
Constant	-.52200	-.51800	-.74000	-.50400	-.71700	-.59500	-.47700	-.46700	-.76600	-.25200	-.36100
Popularity control	1.04300	1.06500	1.04300	1.06200	1.07100	1.10200	.99800	1.01400	1.02200	1.32200	.65500
	(.666)*	(.649)*	(.439)*	(.766)*	(.498)*	(.710)*	(.535)*	(.578)*	(.575)*	(.069)	(.190)*
Sex	.03508	.01430	.03694	.08850	.06167	.01857	.02259	.01203	-.01265	-.03444	-.02677
	(.024)	(.011)	(.030)*	(.052)*	(.052)*	(.012)	(.016)	(.010)	(-.009)	(-.044)*	(-.041)*
Age	.00252	.00375	.00622	.00257	.00571	.00354	.00218	.00380	.00765	.00176	.00313
	(.043)*	(.070)*	(.125)*	(.038)*	(.118)*	(.055)*	(.039)*	(.076)*	(.134)*	(.055)	(.117)*
Graduate degree	.01486	.03465	.04153	.04278	.03755	.03285	.01912	.01798	.03661	-.01061	.02651
	(.010)	(.026)*	(.033)*	(.025)*	(.031)*	(.054)	(.014)	(.014)	(.025)	(-.013)	(.040)*
General author knowledge	.35800	.31500	.39800	.29400	.37700	.37400	.36900	.28000	.39900	.15400	.44100
	(.260)*	(.250)*	(.340)*	(.183)*	(.334)*	(.249)*	(.283)*	(.242)*	(.196)*	(.211)*	(.707)*
Netters	.03443	.02602	.04307	.02762	.03475	.01396	-.00516	.02590	.02861	.01151	.02306
	(.022)	(.018)	(.033)*	(.015)	(.027)*	(.008)	(-.004)	(.020)	(.019)	(.014)	(.033)*
Movers	.01293	.00281	.03097	.03280	.01936	.02086	.00579	.01632	.01937	-.00751	.00155
	(.009)	(.002)	(.025)	(.019)	(.016)	(.013)	(.004)	(.013)	(.014)	(-.010)	(.002)
Moving into region	-.07024	.01331	-.05092	-.12200	-.12900	-.12700	-.13400	-.14300	-.03804	—	—
	(-.020)	(.004)	(-.020)	(-.029)	(-.080)*	(-.034)	(-.050)*	(-.064)*	(-.019)		

New England	**.18200**	−.01147	.02225	−.01461	−.03349	−.01279	−.06880	−.03566	−.03858	−.04494	.01061
	(.071)*	(−.005)	(.009)	(−.004)	(−.015)	(−.004)	(−.026)	(−.015)	(−.014)	(−.038)	(.009)
Middle Atlantic	−.00698	**.06941**	.03411	−.03550	−.00962	−.00676	−.08116	−.05993	−.00626	−.05493	−.02628
	(−.003)	**(.038)***	(.018)	(.013)	(.005)	(−.003)	(−.038)*	(−.032)*	(−.003)	(−.056)	(−.026)*
East North Central	−.01215	−.04875	**.14900**	.00072	−.04092	.00586	−.06443	−.04463	−.00915	−.06091	−.01857
	(−.006)	(−.027)	**(.094)***	(.000)	(−.025)	(.003)	(−.034)*	(−.027)	(−.005)	(−.067)	(−.021)*
West North Central	−.01812	−.05180	.00760	**.22600**	−.03121	−.01742	−.01313	−.02971	−.02783	−.03358	−.01039
	(−.007)	(−.020)	(.003)	**(.077)***	(−.014)	(−.006)	(−.005)	(−.013)	(−.010)	(−.029)	(−.008)
South Atlantic	−.03411	.02276	−.01544	−.04316	**.20100**	.00841	−.02896	−.06180	−.00686	−.05511	−.01102
	(−.020)	(.014)	(−.010)	(−.021)	**(.146)***	(.004)	(−.018)	(−.042)*	(−.004)	(−.065)	(−.014)
East South Central	.00257	.03858	−.02682	−.04624	.07198	**.22500**	.02506	−.03568	−.02766	−.06206	.00249
	(.001)	(.013)	(−.010)	(−.012)	(.027)	**(.076)***	(.008)	(−.013)	(−.009)	(−.048)	(.002)
West South Central	.00509	.01250	−.03855	−.03297	−.00262	.03143	**.30200**	−.05042	−.00590	−.06578	.00776
	(.002)	(.005)	(−.002)	(−.011)	(−.001)	(.012)	**(.148)***	(−.024)	(−.002)	(−.058)	(.007)
Mountain	.00279	−.01549	−.01503	.00711	−.03203	.00043	.02477	**.33200**	−.01136	−.06682	.01854
	(.001)	(−.007)	(−.007)	(.003)	(−.016)	(.000)	(.011)	**(.170)***	(−.005)	(−.060)	(.017)
Pacific	−.03411	−.02110	−.03088	.00444	−.01302	−.05552	−.01559	.01403	**.14900**	−.07231	−.00830
	(−.019)	(−.012)	(−.020)	(.002)	(−.009)	(−.027)	(−.009)	(.009)	**(.092)***	(−.087)*	(−.010)
R²	*.535*	*.494*	*.346*	*.639*	*.416*	*.569*	*.387*	*.417*	*.460*	*.150*	*.637*
N of cases	*9,800*	*8,609*	*9,855*	*8,471*	*10,701*	*7,058*	*8,078*	*10,106*	*8,644*	*1,747*	*11,791*

Note: Respondents are Survey2000 participants with a bachelor's degree or more education. Numbers in parentheses are standardized regression coefficients. Boldface numbers are those critical to the text.

* denotes significant at p < .001

regardless of what region the authors are identified with (the "cosmopolitan" hypothesis). Second, we can test competing hypotheses regarding the differences between movers and stayers within the region of interest. On the one hand is the "deep-roots" hypothesis, which states that movers may know more about authors in general than do stayers, but stayers will know more about their own region's authors than the movers into the region will. On the other hand, movers may catch up to stayers or even surpass them when it comes to knowledge of local regional authors. In this way, movers act like cowbirds, parasitic birds that invade the nests of other birds and make themselves at home there (thus, this is the "cowbirds" hypothesis).

Table 5 reports regression coefficients for regressions of each of the regional dependent variables, namely each respondent's mean recognition score for authors associated with each of the census regions (as well as the mean recognition score for all twenty-eight authors viewed by each respondent). Table 5 also reports the amount of variation explained by all the variables together.

In terms of the variables usually associated with reading, table 5 shows few surprises. General knowledge of literature is strongly positively associated with regional literary knowledge. Having a graduate degree and being female generally increases literary knowledge, though many of these differences are trivial. And older adults know consistently more than younger ones. More surprisingly, our data generally show a small but positive association between familiarity with the Internet ("Netters") and knowledge of regional authors.

The most striking finding in table 5 is that respondents who live in any region definitively recognize the authors from that region significantly more than respondents who live outside the region. The regionalism hypothesis is thus strongly supported.[16]

16. Though many of these educational effects are trivial, when these regressions were done without limiting respondents to the college educated, education was a very strong positive predictor, though usually not as strong as was living in the region.

Disentangling the mobility hypotheses is a bit more difficult because it necessitates taking into account both the interaction and additive coefficients. The additive regression coefficient for the "Movers" variable refers to the difference between movers and stayers who do not live in the region of interest. Thus, it is a good test of the cosmopolitan hypothesis. Movers who do not live in the region do generally know more than stayers who do not live in the region. Though these differences are small, they do support the cosmopolitan hypothesis.

Assessing the deep-roots and cowbirds hypotheses (which can be seen as being on a continuum depending on the gradient of how much movers into a region catch up to those who were born there and live there currently) is achieved by adding the "Movers" additive coefficient to the "Moving into Region" interaction coefficient (e.g., respondents who moved into New England have average recognition scores for New England authors that are .05731 lower than those born there who still live there; movers into the Middle Atlantic score .01612 higher than stayers, etc.). This yields three different groups of regions, different from each other only by gradient of the difference between movers and stayers who both live in the region currently: (1) In Middle Atlantic, East North Central, and Pacific, there are virtually no differences between movers and stayers who live in those regions when it comes to recognizing authors associated with those regions. These are clear "cowbirds" regions. Movers catch up to stayers or surpass them. (2) Movers into New England and West North Central lag slightly behind those born there in recognizing their regional authors, though these differences are still not statistically significant. These are cowbirds regions where the movers nearly catch up to stayers. (3) The three southern regions (South Atlantic, East South Central, and West South Central) and Mountain fall somewhere between the cowbirds and the deep-roots theories. Movers into these regions lag behind those born there and still living there in their recognition of their regional authors, yet movers into these regions still recognize their regional authors significantly better than both movers and stayers who live outside their region.[17]

In sum, table 5 confirms strongly and definitively that where people live affects whom they read. People are much more likely to recognize authors from a region if they live there, and this is the case for all nine regions. Regional culture endures. Moving in general seems to enhance the likelihood of knowing all authors slightly. We take this to support the cosmopolitan effect: movers know more about all authors, even regionalists. For any specific region, people born there initially know more about the local authors than newcomers do. This is hardly surprising; the surprise is that in five out of nine regions, the newcomers catch up completely or almost completely, and in the remaining four regions they are not too far behind. Deep roots matter, but people are cultural cowbirds as well.

Cosmopolitans and Cowbirds

Movers usually know about as much about the literature of the region they currently live in as do the people who have always lived there. In other words, newcomers turn into regionalists just like the old-timers. There are two likely explanations for this: One is that movers are cosmopolitans, people whose travels have made them more knowledgeable about everything. The second is that movers are cowbirds, people who come in and absorb the cultural characteristics of their new homes, just as cowbirds infiltrate and thrive in the nests made by other birds. These two possibilities are not mutually exclusive.

Movers as a whole do seem to be cosmopolitans. They are somewhat more educated than stayers. Even holding education

---

17. Middle Atlantic movers score .01612 points higher. East North Central movers score .01995 points lower. Pacific movers score .01867 points lower. New England movers score .05731 points lower. West North Central movers score .0892 points lower. South Atlantic movers score .10964 points lower. East South Central movers score .10614 points lower. West South Central movers score .12821 points lower. Mountain movers score .12668 points lower.

constant, they seem to pick up cultural savvy with each move. As table 3 indicates, stayers don't show any pattern of cultural acquisition, while movers seem to acquire more knowledge of their local literatures as they age. They are exposed to more cultural influences, in other words, and some of them stick. At the same time, the cosmopolitanism of movers is rather weak and very general, so it cannot explain the variation between particular regions and states.[18]

In the majority of cases, movers act like cultural cowbirds as well. They move right into the new nest, make themselves at home, and flourish on the cultural nourishment surrounding them in that place. Developing a local literary knowledge, they catch up with the stayers. At the regional level, as we saw in table 5, this happens in five out of nine regions.

The cowbird effect can operate at the state level as well. Consider Maine, which (as chapter 5 will demonstrate) has an unusually strong literary culture. Movers currently living in Maine have roughly the same knowledge of regional (New England) authors as stayers. But when we look at their knowledge of Maine authors, as shown in table 6, we see that movers know as much about the state's authors as native Mainers do. And this doesn't seem to be just because these movers are cosmopolitans; they don't know much about the authors from their birth states and they know less about the authors from where they lived in their youth than they do about the authors from Maine, where they live now. In other words, they have operated as cultural cowbirds, moving into a new cultural region and developing knowledge of the local literary world that equals that of the lifelong residents.[19]

18. The mean education score for movers was 5.60 (N = 10,074), while for stayers it was 5.00 (N = 11,215).

19. Of current Maine residents with a bachelor's degree or higher, movers have a New England authors recognition score of .9917, while the score for stayers is 1.0713. Recall that "stayer" and "mover" refer to region, not state, so the numbers change even for the stayers, since some stayers have moved to different states in their home regions. For both movers and stayers, we see a dip at age 21. We suspect that this is the result of people who reside in a state during college years (e.g., in the case of a regional stayer,

TABLE 6 Average state author recognition scores for stayers and movers currently living in Maine

Respondent's age	Mobility	
	Stayers	Movers
Birth	1.1158	.6690
	(.5415)	(.6340)
Age 14	1.0103	.8938
	(.5372)	(.5773)
Age 21	.9113	.8922
	(.6148)	(.6409)
Current	1.1486	1.1389
	(.6825)	(.6137)

Note: Respondents are Survey2000 participants with a bachelor's degree or more education. The four time points under age indicate when the respondent lived in the state he or she claimed. Numbers in parentheses are standard deviations.

The case of Maine raises the possibility that in some states, just as in some regions, newcomers make themselves at home culturally by catching up with natives' knowledge of the local writers. Migrating birds, in other words, act like cowbirds. A state-by-state comparison of state-level stayers' and movers' recognition scores bears this out. Slight differences between the recognition scores, lack of proper controls, and in some cases small numbers of cases, caution one from drawing conclusions about individual states, but we can say this: in most regions (New England, Middle Atlantic, East North Central, West North Central, South Atlantic, Pacific, and Alaska), around half of the states contain educated movers who know more about the state's authors than educated stayers. Movers are not just catching up with stayers, but may even be surpassing them. The exceptions are West South Central, Mountain, and East South Central, where the movers don't seem as inclined to catch up.

---

the student from Massachusetts who attends Bowdoin College in Maine), but do not absorb the state's local literary culture.

How do the different regions compare with one another in terms of their literary cultures? If movers are cosmopolitans, when do they go further and become literary cowbirds, culturally at home and as local as the locals, and where does this fail to happen? We are going to look at this on a regional basis, comparing the regions in terms of their movers' and stayers' knowledge of regional authors.

In order to compare regions we must first take account of the fact that some regions have produced better-known authors than others—recall the large number of New England authors on the top ten lists. So pulling together what we learned from tables 4 and 5, we have examined the regions to see (1) how widely recognized their authors are, and (2) how recognized they are by the residents of the region in question.

The data from table 4 suggest that West North Central and New England are the regions with the best-known authors, and in both of these cases the residents know their authors extremely well. The next tier of regions, whose authors are fairly well known, includes East South Central, West South Central, and Pacific. The latter two of these follow the pattern of West North Central and New England: the residents know their authors considerably better than nonresidents do. East South Central appears anomalous in table 4, for the residents seem to know their region's authors not more, but actually less than nonresidents do. This anomaly is corrected in table 5, where the addition of the popularity controls reveals that East South Central residents do in fact know their region's authors better than nonresidents. The third tier—Middle Atlantic, East North Central, South Atlantic, and Mountain—includes those regions whose authors are least well known overall. Despite their relative obscurity, however, the regions' residents know them considerably better than outsiders do.[20]

20. Recall that not all respondents saw the same set of authors from each region, and living in the region made one inclined to see more authors from that region. What happened with East South Central was that nonresidents saw fewer East South Central authors, and thus the impact of some of their more well-known authors (such as

Dynamic Endurance

Literary regionalism is alive and well. This chapter has demonstrated this empirically. Not only is regionalism flourishing, but also residential mobility—one of the dynamic processes that has been thought to erode regionalism—may actually be strengthening it.

Some insight about how literary regionalism reproduces comes from looking at young people. Many institutions—including libraries, festivals, state humanities councils, local author associations, state "Centers for the Book," and especially schools— function to reproduce the association between literature and a particular place. Children learn the connection between place and literature at school. All states require their students be taught their state's history in either late primary school or middle school, and teachers will frequently pursue language-arts and history objectives in tandem. For example, according to the Arizona Department of Education's Social Studies standards, fourth and fifth grade students focus on Arizona and are expected to:

> Describe the economic, social, and political life in the Arizona Territory and the legacy of various cultural groups to modern Arizona, with emphasis on: how Arizona became a part of the United States through the Mexican Cession and the Gadsden Purchase; the conflict of cultures that occurred between newcomers and Arizona Indian groups, including the Indian Wars; the lives and contributions of various cultural and ethnic groups, including American Indians, Hispanics, and newcomers from the United States and other parts of the world; the importance and contributions of various occupations to the growing Arizona communities, including soldiers (Buffalo soldiers), miners, merchants, freighters, homemakers, ranchers, cowboys, farmers, and railroad workers.[21]

William Faulkner and Tennessee Williams) inflated their averages. East South Central residents who saw many more authors from this region did not have the benefit of such inflation. This problem is corrected in the multivariate regressions in table 5 through the "Popularity Control" variable.

21. Arizona Department of Education. *Social Studies Standards.* "Standard 1: History." Taken from http://www.ade.state.az.us/standards/sstudies/standard.1.

The emphasis on Southwest history continues in the middle and high school standards, which stipulate a more complex understanding of the Western expansion and (among other things) its impact on Native Americans.

The Arizona Department of Education does not select the actual books its students read; states almost never mandate particular titles, which are more often chosen by districts or individual teachers. Since certain works of fiction reinforce history lessons while achieving reading goals as well, however, Arizona teachers or districts often will select a book like Scott O'Dell's *Sing Down the Moon* (1970). This children's classic tells of the 1860 relocation of the Navajo from Canyon de Chelly in Arizona to Fort Sumner in New Mexico as seen through the eyes of a fourteen-year-old girl. *Sing Down the Moon* was a New York Times Outstanding Book of the Year, is available in multiple editions, and appeals to diversity-minded educators. Furthermore, it is featured in a resource book put out by Scholastic for middle-school teachers, *35 Best Books for Teaching U.S. Regions: Using Fiction to Help Students Explore the Geography, History, and Cultures of the Seven U.S. Regions—and Link Literature to Social Studies.* As the subtitle suggests, many teachers and school districts, making independent choices, do chose and use fiction in this way. Younger students may find *G Is for Grand Canyon: An Arizona Alphabet* in their classrooms, while high school English teachers and librarians may steer them to Barbara Kingsolver's *The Bean Trees* or Gregory McNamee's *Named in Stone and Sky: An Arizona Anthology.* The Arizona example demonstrates one way that students learn to associate their state or region with works of literature.[22]

But does such instruction actually take hold? A separate module of Survey2000 was given to children, ages 12–16. Children saw a list of ten books. Unlike in the adult survey, each child saw the same list, and they saw titles, not authors. They indicated whether or not they had heard of or read each of the titles. Thus

---

22. *35 Best Books for Teaching U.S. Regions* is by Buzzeo and Kurtz (2002). *G Is for Grand Canyon* (Gowan and Larson 2002) is part of the "Alphabet Series" available for many states.

we have recognition scores comparable to those of the adult respondents.

Of the ten books, we considered five to be clearly and unambiguously regional in that they were set in and emphasized the way of life in a particular region. These were Esther Forbes's *Johnny Tremain* (Massachusetts, New England), Laura Ingalls Wilder's *Little House on the Prairie* (Kansas, West North Central), Scott O'Dell's *Carlotta* (California, Pacific), Gary Paulson's *Canyons* (New Mexico, Mountain), and Harper Lee's *To Kill a Mockingbird* (Alabama, East South Central). We looked to see which regions had the highest recognition scores for each book, hypothesizing that no matter how well known the book was overall, regional books would be especially well known in their home regions.[23]

This children-as-regionalists hypothesis—youth knowing the children's classics of their region especially well—was born out in four out of the five cases. As table 7 shows, young people do seem to be absorbing the regional literature appropriate to their age. The exception was *To Kill a Mockingbird*, which is read more by our West Coast respondents than by those from its home region of the East South Central (its author, Harper Lee, was from Alabama, and the story takes place there). And while the second place in recognition did go to East South Central, the adjacent Southern region (West South Central) was dead last. While fragmentary, this evidence together with the data on movers suggests the possibility that the new Southerners of the New South—those who are moving there and those who have been born there in recent years—may not be the regionalists that their predecessors and parents have been. But outsider members

23. A sixth, *Huckleberry Finn*, might also be associated with West North Central because of Mark Twain, although we doubted if this would be much of a factor, since much of the story takes place outside of that region, in fact in the South. As it happens, *Huckleberry Finn* has its highest recognition rate in the Pacific region. Beverly Cleary's *Ramona the Pest* takes place in the Pacific Northwest, but this is a minor theme and we did not expect much regional variation. Nor did we expect much from J. D. Salinger's *Catcher in the Rye*, which takes place around New York. We also had two series, Goosebumps and American Girl, which are not associated with particular places.

TABLE 7 Recognition of children's books, by readers' region*

	Little House on the Prairie	Johnny Tremain	Carlotta	Canyons	To Kill a Mockingbird
New England	1.41	.77*	.32	.41	.91
Middle Atlantic	1.29	.48	.27	.32	.81
East North Central	1.35	.41	.25	.39	.84
West North Central	1.44*	.64	.28	.43	.81
South Atlantic	1.31	.57	.28	.36	.91
East South Central	1.39	.74	.19	.35	.95
West South Central	1.33	.42	.28	.42	.77
Mountain	1.38	.55	.32	.44*	.89
Pacific	1.41	.64	.36*	.43	1.03*

* Highest recognition score for each title.

of the reading class (Californians!) know Southern writers, and they teach their children about them.

Overall, regional literature endures in America, despite mobility, despite homogenization, despite electronic media, despite swatches of sprawl, despite globalization, and despite the peculiarities of each region. It is being reproduced internally, as regions indoctrinate both children and newcomers into the local literary traditions. It is also being reproduced externally, as in the cases of the paradoxical regionalism whereby outsiders know the regional writers almost as well as the insiders do. Members of the reading class—be they cowbirds, cosmopolitans, or natives—know, read, and promote regional authors.

Can such regionalism be considered authentic? Cultural history, like all history, is as much a matter of what to forget as of what to remember, so there is no question that today's regionalism is selective. In this respect regionalism is what Raymond Williams would have called emergent culture, produced and reproduced by cowbirds as well as by locals (although we suspect that something like this has always been the case). It is also a product of movement, a result of dynamic rather than static populations. People moving into an area do not live out of their suitcases, culturally speaking. In most cases they settle in, they make themselves at home, they become regionalists. Being a knowledgeable local is not at the opposite pole from being a cosmopolitan, as the old dichotomy had it. Instead, attaining local cultural knowledge is one of the ways people enact and demonstrate their cosmopolitanism.[24]

For members of the reading class, regionalism itself is a requirement for and consequence of participating in world culture. Identities are more a matter of choice than they traditionally were, but that doesn't mean they are any less important. For some people, regionalism is a matter of habit, for others a matter of conviction, and for others regionalism is a choice. Just as people may decide to celebrate their ethnicity or their national background, many choose to celebrate their place, be it ancestral or new. The practices guided by such implicit decisions and such habits—practices including what books to buy, to read, to teach, to talk about, to remember—are the ongoing and dynamic processes that maintain and recreate enduring regional cultures.

24. For a wide-ranging discussion of how forgetting most of the past is absolutely necessary for remembering any of it, see Lowenthal (1985).

4

Paradox in Italy[1]

Cultural regionalism endures when readers and regionalist literature connect with each other. So far we have seen that the regional impulse, the desire for a sense of place, remains strong, and this impulse supports various expressions of cultural regionalism such as cuisine, language, folk customs, dress, festivals, and literature. Literature expresses place through content (the pastoral-derived regionalist aesthetic), through intention (regionalist cultural movements), and through framing (classification and association of authors with a particular place). When an active and committed reading class seeks regionalist materials, as in the United States, literary regionalism is robust, and may indeed be an emergent cultural phenomenon more than a residual one.

At the same time, such literary regionalism is not inevitable. Neither aesthetic content nor authorial intention can produce it if the reading class does not support it. Two things are necessary to make the connection between the reading class and regionalist

1. An earlier version of this chapter appeared in 2000 as "Lo sradicamento: il regionalismo letterario e il paradosso italiano," *Polis: Recerche e Studi su Società e Politica in Italia* XIV, no. 2 (2000): 191–211. *Polis* is published at the University of Bologna, Italy.

literature: First, there must be a literary system that provides the infrastructure for framing and promoting books in terms of their regional significance. This is a matter of the economics of publishing, the prestige hierarchies of writers, and the type of distributive infrastructure in place. Second, there must be a sufficient proportion of the relevant reading class that desires regional literature. This is a matter of the numbers and locations of readers, and of the politics of reading.

This chapter looks at Italy, a country that presents a paradox: political, economic, and cultural regionalism are intense, yet literary regionalism is surprisingly weak. The Italian case reveals the types of structural and political filters that, despite favorable cultural conditions, can prevent literary regionalism from emerging.

In Italian literature, staying in place seems to be difficult. Boccaccio's young people flee plague-ridden Florence for the Fiesole hills; Manzoni's unlucky lovers are driven from their village by the lustful Don Rodrigo; Carlo Levi's northern intellectual endures exile in a southern village so desolate that even Christ hadn't made it there; Elsa Morante's Iduzza and Useppe are tossed from one shaky refuge to another by the vicissitudes of war; Umberto Eco's Franciscan official travels from England to sort things out in the monastery. Italian masterpieces are remarkably concerned with displacement. Although Italy is said to be a country where local attachments are so strong that people feel homesick if they go beyond the sound of their village bells, classic and contemporary Italian literature features people profoundly out of place.[2]

These refugees, nomads, and exiles embody the Italian paradox of place. In a country where geography is fundamental to social, political, and economic life, and where individual writers have produced regionalist classics like *The Day of the Owl,*

2. The works referred to are Giovanni Boccaccio's *Il Decameron* (1359–51; revised 1370–72); Alessandro Manzoni's *I promessi sposi* (1827; *The Betrothed*); Carlo Levi's *Cristo se è fermato a Eboli* (1945; *Christ Stopped at Eboli*); Elsa Morante's *La Storia* (1974; *History: A Novel*); and Umberto Eco's *Il nome della rosa* (1980; *The Name of the Rose*).

nevertheless Italian writers seldom organize themselves on a regional basis and Italian writing is seldom published, anthologized, taught, celebrated, or sold according to regional classifications. In a nation where cultural regionalism is rampant, literary regionalism is rare. The reading class, although emotionally attached to place, neither produces nor demands regional writing. In such a situation where a robust culture of place already exists, the puzzle is, why does Italy's vibrant regionalism find such weak literary expression?

Probing the Italian puzzle requires an institutional look at the production of cultural regionalism. When does the celebration of a region or locality energize the literary field, and when does it fail to attain momentum? Approaching this question begins with the recognition that culture is not autonomous, not the ineffable result of chance and genius, experience shaped by inspiration, but instead is the product of political struggles, organizational arrangements, and economic flows. These production elements, we shall demonstrate, shape how and indeed whether a culture of place finds expression in literature.[3]

3. That culture results from people pursuing economic and political as well as cultural goals is now widely accepted, but this idea has had a stormy history. Following World War II, the Frankfurt School attitude toward culture industries held sway. Horrified by the image of societies mesmerized by totalitarian ideologues, Theodor Adorno, Max Horkheimer, Leo Lowenthal, and their colleagues warned against culture's capacity to stupefy the populace by offering it mindless entertainment. The "culture industry" consisted of profit-seeking firms that created and marketed cultural objects, producing a mass culture that both brutalized audiences and reduced their capacity for critical social analysis. Intellectuals of both the left and the right regarded culture, formerly a domain of freedom, as being under assault by its reduction to just another commodity rolling off the assembly line.

Cultural revolutions of the 1960s, including the rise of youth cultures, stimulated sociologists to rethink the politics and mechanics of cultural production. This reappraisal ultimately shattered the assumed links between culture as product and culture as threat. Developments in organizational sociology led the way to a politically neutral investigation of the creation and dissemination of cultural objects. At the same time, developments in media studies, in semiotics, and in reception aesthetics drew attention to the fact that the impact of such cultural objects derived less from what the producers intended than from how the receivers interpreted the cultural artifacts in question. By the middle of the 1970s the "production of culture" and the "culture industries" had lost

Cultural Regionalism without Literary Regionalism

Regions are key to understanding Italy. Descriptions of Italian geography, culture, economics, politics, history, dialects, customs, and cuisine are invariably conceived in terms of regions. And unlike in the United Kingdom, Spain, and other much-discussed sites of European regionalism where the "regions" are typically thought of as a few places on the periphery, like Catalonia or northern England, in Italy the regions cover the entire country. It is commonly said that Italians identify more strongly with their local places of origin than with the nation-state, regarding themselves more as Sicilians or Tuscans or Venetians than as Italians.[4]

While regionalism is invoked constantly, there is no general agreement on just what the regions of Italy are. At least six ways of dividing up Italian regions are common: (1) the twenty administrative regions, as shown in figure 8; (2) the basic North/South split; (3) the three ISTAT (Istituto Nazionale di Statistica) regions of Nord, Centro, and Mezzogiorno; (4) the five ISTAT regions (ISTAT sometimes splits the Northeast from the Centro, and further splits the Islands); (5) the "three Italies" in the literature on industrial districts and flexible specialization (the

---

their pejorative connotations, having come to refer to the organizational apparatus for discovering, fabricating, and marketing cultural goods. At about the same time, related developments effaced the distinction between "high" and "mass" culture. In England the Birmingham School of Cultural Studies showed that popular culture —women's magazines, teenage styles—retained the capacity for critical engagement with the social order. Sociologists and historians showed that high/low differentiation was a relatively recent development that had more to do with social snobbery than with characteristics of the cultural objects so stratified. These developments represented a more dispassionate approach to empirical cultural analysis. Classical formulations of the production of culture approach include Hirsch (1972), Peterson (1976, 1978), and Becker (1982). For the relationship between social stratification and definitions of high and low culture, see Bourdieu (1979), Burke (1978), and Levine (1988). For some of the institutional infrastructure of cultural sociology, see Griswold (1993).

4. Note that I am using regions in the general sense of a place, a territory distinct from other territories, and not necessarily in the specific sense of the twenty Italian *regioni*. For overviews of Italian regionalism, see Cento Bull (2000) and Levy (1996).

FIGURE 8. Map of Italy's twenty regions

backward South; the heavy-industry Northwest; and the dynamic, small-enterprise Center and Northeast; (6) geographical regions, sometimes broken down as mountains, hills, and plains, and sometimes continental, peninsular, and insular.[5]

5. The twenty regioni break down as follows. There are seven regions included in the North (Nord): Italia Nord-occidentale (Northwest) includes Valle d'Aosta, Lombardia, Piemonte, and Liguria. Italia Nord-orientale (Northeast) includes Friuli-Venezia

Localism in the form of the practical and cultural penumbra surrounding a city constitutes yet another type of regionalism. Cities and towns have distinctive cultural characteristics (dialect, cuisine) and are at the hub of social networks and institutions that can be mobilized for economic and political ends. The circulation of Italian newspapers is far more local than national. Localism is often present on an even smaller scale—a particular neighborhood, quarter, or parish—the urban equivalent of the within-the-sound-of-the-bells village provincialism.[6]

Regions, as we saw in chapter 1, are not facts, but geographic fictions put to social uses. As Michael Keating puts it, "A region is a construction, of history and of present day actions. Its invention depends on the confluence of these distant meanings of space." So there is not some fixed set of Italian regions. Nevertheless, scholars, cultural enthusiasts, and Italians constantly invoke regions of one sort or another to describe how Italy works.[7]

Although the popular and scholarly attention paid to regions in Italy implies that regional literary culture would be robust, in fact this is not the case. Although certain writers can be considered regionalists, nevertheless regional schools or movements are rare. Moreover, regionalism and regional classifications have played

---

Giulia, Trento Alto-Aldige, and Veneto. Italia Centrale (Central) includes Emilia-Romagna, Toscana, Umbria, Marche, and Abruzzi. Lazio (Rome) is sometimes separated. Italia Meridionale (South, often called the Mezzogiorno) includes Molise, Campania, Calabria, Basilicata, and Puglia. Italia Insulare (the Islands)—Sicilia and Sardegna—are usually included in the Mezzogiorno, but sometimes separated.

For the "three Italies," see Trigilia (1992); the tri-partite division originated with Bagnasco (1977). Paul Ginsborg, who has done more than anyone else to bring contemporary Italian history and society to an English-speaking readership, offers yet another variation: Bagnasco's "three Italies"—Northwest; Northeast and Center; and South and the Islands—plus a fourth, Lazio, which he treats as "a case apart because of the predominance of Rome in that region, with its consequent distorting effect upon regional statistics" (2003, 325).

6. Data from 1971 show that for the larger Italian newspapers, 75–95 percent of their circulation was in their own region; even *Il Corriere della Sera*, the one paper that claimed a national market, had two-thirds of its market in Lombardy (Forgacs 1990a).

7. "A region is a construction . . ." quotation is from Keating (1997, 10). Robert Putnam's (1993) study of variations in civic culture based on long-existing regional patterns is a well-known example.

virtually no part in the discursive organization of Italian litera-ture. Most discussions of twentieth-century Italian literature, for example, include categories such as hermeticism, neorealism, the neo-avantgarde (Gruppo 63), and feminist writers, but not cat-egories like "Mezzogiorno writers" or "voices from the Third Italy." In contrast, just about any broad treatment of twentieth-century American literature would include a section on Southern writers and might also include a separate category for writers from the West.

To say that regionalism plays little role in the organization of Italian literature is in reference to how literature is packaged and categorized by its producers and its consumers. Regional-ism does play a role in some literary criticism. For example, in the mid-twentieth century the critic Carlo Dionisotti reacted to Croce's neo-idealism by stressing the historical and geographical influences on Italian writers, and in the late 1980s, Alberto Asor Rosa analyzed the tension between unitary and multiple centers of literary production.[8] Despite these occasional scholarly ap-proaches, however, from the point of view of the typical reader, things look quite different. Very few regional anthologies exist. Bookstores and libraries do not separate out the writers from or literature about the local region (although they may separate out regional cookbooks or travel guides). University literature courses specific to a certain region are all but unknown. And in an ex-ception that proves the rule, the one compendium I have found that organizes its discussion of Italian literature around regions was written by two Germans![9]

Many masterpieces of Italian writing, as was seen in *The Day of the Owl,* are very specific in terms of their physical and social settings. *Il Gattopardo (The Leopard)* is imagined in and through Sicilian social structure, *I Promessi Sposi* is faithful to accounts of seventeenth-century Milan and Lecco, and it makes a difference

8. Asor Rosa (1989).
9. Literary criticism that is organized around the regional backgrounds of authors includes: Giglio (1995); Stussi (1979); Dionisotti (1967); Asor Rosa (1989). The com-pendium is Maurer and Maurer (1993).

that Christ stopped in Eboli and not in Venice. But such masterpieces were not a part of, and did not give rise to, regionalist schools of writing or regionalist movements. Moreover, they are held to be common Italian property. Secondary-school students in the south and the north equally work their way through Manzoni, for example; he is not seen as a "northern writer," and at least so far the Northern League has not claimed ownership of him.

Saying that Italy lacks regional literature, therefore, by no means implies that the country has no regionalist writers. A regionalist writer is someone who writes about a region; in the ideal typical case, that writer comes from a region, writes about it, is associated with it by outsiders, and is honored within it. Just to take Sicily as a convenient example, Giuseppe Tomasi di Lampedusa (*The Leopard*) was a regionalist writer; so was Leonardo Sciascia; so is the contemporary mystery writer Andrea Camilleri, whose Inspector Montalbano's relationship with his Genovese lover is conflicted in large part because of their regional habits of mind.[10]

The presence of some regionalist writers does not create a regional literature, however. Literary regionalism is a social construct, not an aggregation of individual phenomena. It takes the form of either a cultural movement from within a region or a cultural frame imposed from without. On the one hand, regional literature as a movement typically results from a group of writers who want to give voice to their region's distinctiveness and/or to document a vanishing way of life. Local intellectuals, who may perceive themselves as disadvantaged by language and/or ethnicity, by poverty, or by distance from metropolitan centers, will frequently generate such a cultural movement. On the other hand, if writers from some area get clustered together in an anthology of "Voices from the West," for example, or if universities teach courses on Western literature, this is a case of regionalist literature by external framing. Sometimes such a framing takes hold,

---

10. See Brand and Pertile (1996, 590–93), for discussion of some regional writers of the 1970s.

and sometimes it doesn't. The relationship between movement and frame are often interactive; regardless of whether it has been triggered by a cultural movement or an external framing, once a regional literature exists as a broadly accepted subgenre, it is hard for a writer from the region to avoid the label.

Regional literature as a movement or frame, therefore, does not arise from just one or two people writing about the region and its people. Pier Paolo Pasolini wrote poetry in the Fruilian dialect, but his activities do not amount to a Fruilian regional literature; there was no cultural movement among Fruilian writers (Pasolini himself moved on), nor has there been a subsequent framing of a Fruilian School. Tomasi di Lampedusa wanted to document a vanishing world, not to establish a Sicilian literary movement—and neither did Leonardo Sciascia, described as a "lonely figure." A better case can be made for some pre-unification regionalist movements, such as that surrounding Carlo Porta (1775–1821), who wrote in Milanese dialect and satirized the Lombard nobility, but he saw himself as promoting Romanticism rather than regionalism. Giuseppe Belli would be the best known of the dialect poets, but I have seen no evidence of him regarding himself as involved in a Roman regionalist movement, and later in life he renounced his dialect sonnets.[11]

In the post-unification period, writers from Liguria, on the Northwest coast, come closest to regionalism as a cultural movement. Gina Lagorio is a contemporary Piedmontese regionalist, writing of both the Langhe area of her birth and the Ligurian coast where she has lived. She has written a monograph on an earlier Piedmontese writer, Beppe Fenoglio, who inspired in her the "geographical courage" to write about the Langhe region. Lagorio herself uses landscape prominently, as in her 1979 novel *Fuori scena,* in which a woman flees Rome to regain strength in her hometown in the Langhe. Lagorio is a regionalist through intention, for the author consciously positions herself in a regional

11. Barański (1990). The description of Sciascia as a "lonely figure" comes from Brand and Pertile (1996, 591).

lineage that began as a turn-of-the-century cultural movement. In *La spiaggia del lupo,* her 1977 best-selling novel set in Liguria, Lagorio writes:

> The beauty that she enjoyed brought her back to the dreams of an ancient beauty, when Boine arrived in that corner of the world seeking health for his consumed lungs, or Roccatagliata Ceccardi as he hurried along on the last leg of his march toward the life-saving port of his friend Novaro, his pockets empty, the canary in the cage balancing on his shoulder...

Pietralunga informs us that, "The names mentioned in this passage—Giovanni Boine, Roccatagliata Ceccardi, and Mario Novaro—are poets in the Ligurian tradition. Mario Novaro was also a discoverer of literary talent and publisher of the magazine *La Riviera Ligure,* founded by his older brother, Angelo Silvio Novaro, in 1895." A circle of writers, a literary entrepreneur, a magazine, and finally a heritage that subsequent writers attach themselves: this is regionalism as a fledgling cultural movement.[12]

Such movements are possible in Italy, so the question remains, why are they so rare? Why in a recently unified country with profound differences among its regions—differences in economics, in politics, in language, in history—is there so little collective regionalism as either literary movements (intention) or institutional classification (framing)? In a country that is organized along regional lines in so many respects, why has Italy had so little regional literature?

Examining Italian culture from the late nineteenth to the twenty-first centuries, one can discern five overlapping reasons for this surprising absence of literary regionalism. These can be summarized as the "Five *I*'s": illiteracy; intellectuals; ideologies;

---

12. This discussion is based on Pietralunga (1990), who uses the term "geographical courage." The quotation of Lagorio beginning "The beauty that she enjoyed..." is from p. 81, and is his translation. The quotation beginning "The names mentioned..." is from p. 88. I am grateful to Professor Alessandro Pizzorno, who first made me aware of the Ligurian regionalism. See also Mauri (1989).

industries; and Italy. What follows is a consideration of each of these and how they might interact.

Illiteracy

By Western European standards, Italy had high rates of illiteracy well into the twentieth century. While there had long been an intellectual, cosmopolitan elite, a reading class in the restricted sense, the bourgeois readership—the middle-class heart and soul of modern mass reading—appeared late. The effects of this late development linger on, for while literacy rates in Italy as a whole have caught up to the rest of Europe, reading as a practice has not. In 2003, only 41.4 percent of Italians had read a book for pleasure during the previous year. This figure might be compared to the 1994 OECD study (reported in chapter 2) that found 66 percent of people in advanced economies read a book at least once a month, and to the NEA "Reading at Risk" study that found 56.6 percent of Americans have read a book during the past year. While one must be wary of comparing survey findings, given that they come from different years and pose the question somewhat differently, these suggest what many commentators have observed: Italians read less than other Westerners do.[13]

The ability to read did not develop evenly. Like other forms of disadvantage, illiteracy was historically far higher in the South than in the Center or North. In 1881, for example, only 32 percent of the Piedmontese were illiterate, but 85 percent of the people in Basilicata and Calabria were. Literacy increased throughout Italy, but the North/South gap persisted; by 1951 only 3–4 percent of the people in Piedmont, Lombardy, and Liguria were unable

---

13. Italians' low reading rates have been especially well documented in the case of newspapers. Italy and the U.K. have roughly the same population, yet total sales of all of the major daily newspapers in Italy is less than the sales of either the *Daily Mirror* or *Sun* alone in Britain (Nowell-Smith in Barański and Lumley 1990); the sales of weeklies and monthlies are also low. The Italian book reading rate for 2003 is from ISTAT (2005, 2). The American rate of book reading, which refers to 2002, is from National Endowment of the Arts (2004, 9). The OECD rate is from OECD and Statistics Canada (1994, 105).

read, but Basilicata and Calabria still had illiteracy rates of around 30 percent. The North/South difference in reading continues to this day. This gap meant that the Mezzogiorno, precisely the area that because of its historical disadvantages would be most likely to give rise to a cultural movement based on its distinct experience, was the most handicapped due to its small local reading class and, therefore, small market.[14]

Furthermore, illiteracy refers to a disjunction between oral communication, which virtually all human beings master, and written communication. Some version of this disjunction is a fact of life in Italy. A considerable gap exists between written and oral language, a linguistic discontinuity that separates print from lived experience. "Standard Italian," the Tuscan-based language educated Italians use for formal, written communications, was and remains the literary language, but it has never corresponded with the way most people actually talk. At Unification somewhere between 2.5 and 10 percent of the population knew "Italian," and even today 70 percent of Italians use dialect at least part of the time. Thus literary Italian became formal and somewhat precious, a highly wrought language rooted in a single region's dialect. As a consequence, its development was little influenced by the various changes in regional dialects over the centuries. Standard written Italian today shows little regional variation (a linguist might be able to detect some, but variations are lost on the typical reader). Local dialects are seldom written; when people learn to write and read, they learn to write and read in standard Italian. A few writers have employed dialect—e.g., Belli used Roman dialect—but they have not spearheaded movements. This situation set up an unusually sharp contrast between writing and experience.[15]

14. The historical data is from Forgacs (1990a, 18, table 1.1). The South has always lagged behind the rest of the country in education. For example, in 1991, 21.6% of the residents of Lazio (the region of Rome) had secondary education or beyond, while the Northwest was 23.7%, the Northeast and Center 22.8%, and the South 19.1%. While overall education rates have increased in all regions, the respective position of the four regions has been the same since 1951 (Ginsborg 2003, 350, table 42).

15. The discussion of Italian language is from Lepschy (1990). Recently several popular mystery writers, including Andrea Camilleri and Giuseppe Ferrandino, have

Italy has continued to have a low rate of reading, even in the postwar period. A 1957 survey, at the dawn of the "economic miracle" and after illiteracy was no longer a major problem, revealed that two families in five had virtually no regular contact with printed materials (recall Roberts and Foehr's findings about how having print in their home environments encourages children to read, discussed in chapter 2). By then most Italians had the ability read, but many chose not to do so. The disjunction between the written and the spoken word undoubtedly contributes to this reluctance to read, but it is not the only factor. The relative unpopularity of print media, as reflected in the low newspaper reading even today, is not just a case of potential readers unwilling to decode standard Italian; the robust readership for Monday's *Gazzetta dello Sport* belies any such simple explanation. Nor is it due to a lack of leisure time or disposable income for entertainment, for Italians have plenty of both.[16]

The Italians' disinclination to read may have resulted from Italy's late development of a middle class. The typical European pattern for establishment of mass readership saw the emergence of a large body of bourgeois men and women who were literate (usually through the influence of Protestantism) and who had both time and money. Cultural entrepreneurs developed popular literature and the popular press to satisfy this reading class's demand for entertainment and information. In Italy, however, until the twentieth century, this bourgeois stratum was thin; instead, the Italian reading class was a small, highly educated elite, living alongside a large, illiterate mass of laborers and peasants. By the time a good-sized middle class emerged, far more entertainment media were available than had been the case for their European and North American counterparts earlier. When non-elite Italians learned to read in the early twentieth century, cinema and radio competed with print materials for their attention, with

---

featured some characters speaking in dialect. Doing so is a challenge for the writer, for he or she has to ensure that readers who aren't familiar with the dialect can understand what is going on, so it remains to be seen if this catches on.

16. The 1957 survey is from Caesar and Hainsworth (1984, 16). The *Gazzetta dello Sport* example comes from Nowell-Smith (1996).

television to follow by mid-century. Northern European countries and North America, in contrast, had anywhere from fifty to 150 years of high literacy rates before these competing leisure-time alternatives became available. Thus the reading habit had time to become well established in these areas in a way that it did not in Italy. One consequence of this is that Italy continues to produce less popular reading matter—tabloid newspapers, for example, or formulaic romance novels—than do other Western countries.[17]

Sequencing may also explain why the Mezzogiorno, although it has come close to catching up with the rest of the country in terms of literacy, has a lower rate of reading. Southerners buy far fewer newspapers, magazines, and books than do Italians in the North and Center. This is not simply due to having less disposable income, for Southern families spend almost as much on audiovisual hardware and software as do Italians elsewhere. This supports the sequencing hypothesis: by the time Southerners had the education, money, and leisure to read, print media faced such intense competition from electronic media that these newly literate groups never developed the reading habit.[18]

Intellectuals

Gramsci claimed that Italian intellectuals were simultaneously provincial and cosmopolitan, but not national, in their orientation, and most observers agree. The highly educated elite has

17. According to ISTAT, 75% of Italians were illiterate at the time of Unification (1861), and in 1881 almost two-thirds (62%) were. By 1931 the rate of illiteracy was down to about a quarter (26%), and fell to 14% in 1951 (Forgacs 1990, 18). As long ago as the 1930s Gramsci pointed out the lack of indigenous Italian popular literature, which drove people to foreign works. On the other hand, a robust Italian market does exist for transitional forms such as adult comics and *fotoromanzi* that straddle the gap between visual and print communications. For the classic account of the rise of middle-class readers, see Watt (1957/1974).

18. In 1981, Southern illiteracy was 6.4% (Ginsborg 1990, 440, table 22). The comparisons of spending on print and electronics also comes from Forgacs (1990a, 177, table 8.1).

taken to heart their heritage of being at the center of Western civilization for two millennia. While all Italians take pride in their past, for intellectual elites this pride has taken the form of a humanist idealism exemplified by Benedetto Croce. Although a glorious past can foster a narrow provincialism, Italian intellectuals have tended rather to be internationalist, as is typical of intellectual elites from countries with a relatively thin stratum of highly educated people. Both their humanism and cosmopolitanism are universal in their claims, and thus unfavorable to the promotion of a regional culture, particularistic and local by definition.[19]

Italian intellectuals are also committed to playing a public role. Like their French counterparts, they have generally aspired to being visible, politically active, acting as moral guides and exemplars. This has meant that they have seen themselves as addressing the Italian people as a whole, not some subgroup. Regionalism, particularly in European countries, seems to run counter to this. The contradiction between region and nation is not inevitable. In a federal system like the United States, not only is there no conflict between being a champion of one's local region and being a national figure, but the former reinforces the latter; for example, Faulkner's status as a great Southern writer contributes to his status as a great American writer. In a more highly centralized, but imperfectly united country like Italy, the situation is more zero-sum, as demonstrated by the secessionist impulses of regional political parties like the Northern League. Paradoxically, the very intensity of Italy's regionalism makes it hard for intellectuals and artists to be regionalists.

Furthermore, the belief that writers should be public figures has an unanticipated consequence in terms of gender. Women's writing concentrates on personal and domestic life. Although this is a huge generalization with huge numbers of exceptions, it tends to hold for the majority of women writers anyplace in the

19. As seen in the previous chapter, the cosmopolitan orientation does not necessarily preclude local cultural attachments, although it usually does not align with nationalism; see the discussion in Pollock (2000).

world. It follows that, to the extent that writers are conceived of as public figures addressing public issues, women writers are at a disadvantage and their work is devalued. Italian feminists have repeatedly made the point with respect to Italian writers.

There is an affinity between gender and regionalism. Like women's writing, regionalist writing tends to focus on the private and the local. For that very reason, women writers are often prominent regionalist writers, more prominent in regionalism than in their national literature as a whole; the American local-color movement of the late nineteenth century offers a familiar example of this. An intellectual culture that disadvantages women, as in Italy, disadvantages regionalist writing as well.

What about the local intellectuals, the cultural leaders born and bred in a particular region? In any society, most members of the reading class—writers, people in the book trade, buyers of books, readers of books—come from the middle or upper classes, the social elite. In Italy, however, this elite is split: many intellectuals regard regional elites like landowners or industrialists as a parasitic and degenerate group. This is especially so in the South, long victimized by a land-owning oligarchy and corrupt state interventions. According to the rather Darwinian view articulated by Carlo Levi and believed by many observers, young members of the privileged class in the South who had any ability or ambition left the region. Others have stressed structural constraints such as absentee land ownership and systematic neglect from the state that have trapped both local elites as well as peasants. Regardless of how true this widely held view is, it seems safe to say that local intellectuals with literary aspirations have had to leave their region of origin and head for one of the major cities.

A basic fact of literary life is that it is not easy being an intellectual when there is no place to buy books, no place to talk with other intellectuals, no critical mass of readers, no reading class. "Men of ideas," as Lewis Coser pointed out years ago, are drawn to places where there are other men of ideas, places where there are publishers, universities, artists, coffee houses, museums, theaters, and book stores. These are found in the cities, above all in Milan and Rome. The lack of an intellectual infrastructure was especially true in the South, but the urban migration of intellectuals has been the case all over Italy. Such a pattern of the intellectual out-migration obstructs both the development of a regionalist literary voice on an individual level and the collective action of a locally based group of writers.[20]

Nobel laureate Grazia Deledda (1871–1926) exemplified the pattern of a regionalist writer who migrates to Rome or Milan. Although she was a Sardinian regionalist whose early verismo fiction explored the Sardinian social and physical landscape, she moved permanently to Rome when she was twenty-five. Her writing toward the end of her career was far less regionalist, less rooted in Sardinia, than her earlier work had been. Contemporary writers move to the metropolis as well; even Andrea Camilleri, author of the Sicilian detective novels, lives in Rome. Camilleri shows that one can remain a regionalist without remaining in the region, but for many others their writing gradually moves away from their geographical roots and preoccupations.

Ideology

Twentieth-century ideologies discouraged regionalism. The fundamental ideological divide in postwar Italy until the nineties was between Communism, given political voice through the Partito Comunista Italiano (PCI), and Roman Catholicism, whose party was the Christian Democrats. For all their differences, these two ideologies shared strong universal claims, for indeed they were the political arms of the intellectual-as-exemplar strands discussed above. Thus while certain regions might be dominated by one or the other—the "red belt" around Modena, or the staunch Catholicism of the Veneto—neither ideological cluster could allow its message to take on a regional inflection. Both Catholics and Communists worked hard to promote certain forms of cultural

20. For a discussion of the urban migration pattern, see Mauri (1987). For the support structure needed for "men of ideas," see Coser (1965).

expression, asserting respectively the brotherhood of man or the fraternity of the working classes, but these were distinctly non-regionalist.

The seemingly opposing ideologies of Communism and Catholicism actually had a great deal in common with respect to their paternalistic attitudes toward "the people," particularly the rural, uneducated, "backwards" people. The Catholics saw peasants as noble savages, at peace with God and Nature; this was related to a myth of "the land" as wellspring of Christian and civic virtues, and the city as cesspool of materialism and spiritual degradation. In this highly conservative view, the Church needed to protect these rural innocents from contamination from the city, modernity, and radical politics. Cultural change was to be either resisted or, if that proved impossible, controlled.[21]

For the Communists, the peasants had a claim on an authentic culture. At the same time, they needed to be integrated into modernity, not protected from it, and guided into recognition of their natural alliance with the urban working class. The Communists found themselves in a number of awkward positions with respect to culture. They wanted to awaken the peasants and workers culturally as well as politically, but they saw culture as print culture (culture = books = education). They envisioned a literary, standard-Italian, high-culture cluster of symbolic goods—indistinguishable, in fact, from the culture celebrated by conservative intellectuals—to which the peasants and workers had been denied access. In a somewhat schizophrenic attitude toward popular culture, Communist intellectuals celebrated local folk cultures, which were dying, but deplored the mass culture (television, popular music, Hollywood films) that was growing by leaps and bounds and that "the people" were actively choosing.

Another awkward cultural stance involved gender. The PCI encouraged a public form of cultural engagement. They set up

21. See Allum (1990) for an account of Catholic efforts at cultural control, and Forgacs (1990a, 1990b) for an account of the inconsistencies and contradictions that vexed the Communists' cultural endeavors.

film clubs set up in working-class neighborhoods, where a film's showing would be followed by a discussion led by a PCI leader. They set up book centers, *Centro del Libro Populare,* which provided books and a place for literary discussion. All such venues were intended to raise political consciousness. Participation in such public centers, however, was overwhelmingly male. This view of culture as "public" excluded women's participation and rendered invisible women's popular-culture consumption, such as the reading of romance novels and *fotoromanzas* or watching domestic dramas and soap operas on television, all of which took place in the private sphere. This downgrading of women's culture was another way in which Communist ideology discouraged regionalist forms of expression. Women authors and their topics as a whole were structurally incorrect.[22]

David Forgacs points out that this tendency to love the people's culture while wanting to improve or ignore much of it could be found in prewar Fascism as well. The Fascist government started libraries and reading groups, especially in South, to fill the gaps and to "retrieve cultural spaces" from the left (the Communists would later "retrieve" them back). Thus they took over former local or left-run *biblioteche populari,* set up at the beginning of the century, as they took over the function of "taking books to the people." In contrast with the left, however, they gave these moves a specifically "non-class, nationalist, populist inflection"—nationalist, and emphatically not regionalist.[23]

So if we take "the local" as shorthand for those non-metropolitan regions that were late to industrialize, we might say that the Fascists looked at the local and saw the nation. The Communists looked at the local and saw the working class. The Catholics looked at the local and saw God's children. No group of intellectual or cultural leaders, it seems, looked at the local and saw the local. All three ideological positions celebrated folk cultures

22. Forgacs (1990a, ch. 7) points out that the Communists, by championing art that was social, public, and overtly political over art that dealt with the personal, private, inner life, devalued many women authors.

23. Forgacs (1990a, 60).

but attempted to steer the folk toward a nationalist (Fascism), internationalist (Communism), or universal (Catholicism) level. None of these ideologies gave any platform for regional cultural expression.

Catholicism since the 1960s and Communism since the late 1970s have opened up, becoming more pluralistic and more accepting of a variety of cultural forms. The ideological reshuffling that took place in the 1990s gave rise to the political regionalism of the Northern League. And postmodern intellectuals have drawn attention to identity politics whereby place, region, or the local is not a given, but a resource. So some former ideological barriers to regionalism may have been lowered. Market barriers have not, however, and it is to these that we now turn.

Industry

Culture industries exist to generate a profit. Book publishing, newspaper publishing, cinema, broadcasting: all are looking to make money. While there might be the occasional boutique publishing operation that is some rich man's hobby, the independent filmmaker who cares more for art than ticket sales, or the cultural niche supported by public funding, by and large cultural distribution is shaped by the obdurate fact that resources flow toward that which is profitable.

Three factors influence the profitability of books and other print media in Italy: a relatively low average rate of reading, a relatively small linguistic base, and a relatively high rate of foreign imports. First, the question of reading. Italy's low rate of reading has not been simply a by-product of illiteracy. For example, Forgacs notes that the sales of newspapers were roughly the same in 1915 as in 1980, though illiteracy had all but disappeared in the intervening years. Nor is it the case that the oft-repeated assertion that "gli Italiani leggono poco"—Italians don't read much—tells you anything about any particular Italians, for it is a summary statement of aggregate data that masks enormous geographical differences. Nevertheless, as we have seen, compared with people in other industrialized countries, Italians indeed do not read much.[24]

Not only do Italians not read many books, but also not many people outside of Italy read books in Italian. This linguistic situation is what Stefano Mauri refers to as *"la sfortune di essere piccoli"*—the bad luck of being small—and the consequences for publishers are dramatic. Italy, France, and Britain have similar populations—fifty-odd million in 1980—but that year, the world contained 565 million English speakers, 138 million French speakers, but only 57 million Italian speakers. So Italian publishers have to contend with a low, and unevenly distributed, readership at home and a virtually non-existent one abroad.[25]

Translations are profitable, and many books get translated from Italian into some other language. The Italian strength as an exporter of titles comes first and foremost from books on art. Books dealing with some aspect of Catholicism are also important. Overall, however, Italy is an importer of titles, not an exporter. In 1978, there were 1,819 works translated from some other language into Italian, and 1,558 translated from Italian. This unfavorable balance of translations is especially high with respect to English: that year there were 808 translations of English-language works into Italian, 178 translations from Italian into English. Moreover, it is in the area of literature that the English titles are especially strong, so one might sum up the situation as art books being translated out of Italian into English, while popular and serious literature is being translated from English into Italian. Such competition from foreign imports discourages publishers from bringing out Italian authors, especially writers of fiction. Moreover, while translations of Italian art books etc. into

24. Forgacs (1990a). Mauri (1987). The reading picture looks better if you count sports papers and weekly magazines ranging from *Famiglia cristiana* to *Topolino*, although Italy still lacks the popular readership found in countries that had developed a large market for the popular press before the competition from television (cf. Lumley 1996).

25. Mauri (1987, table 1.3). All three countries currently (2006) have about 60 million people, but the low number of Italian speakers compared with English and French has not changed.

foreign languages keep Italian publishers happy, they would have no direct effect on regionalism (regionalist writing, dependent on detailed local knowledge, is even less likely than other types of books to be translated), although they could have an indirect effect of subsidizing the firms' less profitable titles.[26]

These three factors—low internal reading rates, tiny external market in Italian, and a translation pattern based primarily on books on art and religion as well as a few classic writers like Dante—discourage regionalism. The first two also discourage book publication in general. One comparative indicator presents the situation unmistakably: having comparable populations, France published 32,000 books in 1980; Britain 48,000; and Italy only 13,000.[27]

In many countries local publishers foster regionalism by publishing books by local authors for a local market, but not in Italy. Publishing is highly concentrated in a few firms, mostly in Milan; 20 percent of the publishing houses account for 66 percent of the market. The rest is made up of much smaller publishers, which are geographically scattered. The big firms, with their heavy advertising costs, aim for national markets. As for the smaller firms, they are less driven to seek broad markets (many are family-run enterprises with little expectation of making a profit) and, since they are likely to be located in non-metropolitan areas, one might expect them to play the fostering-local-writing role. However, many are prevented from doing so by the fact that they lack a sufficient local market to support such writing. Mezzogiorno publishers in particular cannot count on a regional readership.[28]

Comparing books with newspapers demonstrates how the regionalist impulse may be encouraged or discouraged by industrial

26. Mauri (1987, table 1.4). Although the translation situation disadvantages literature, nevertheless Dante was one of the top three authors translated in 1978; the others were Emilio Salgari (1862–1911), a prolific author of adventure stories who is often compared to Jules Verne, and Carlo Collodi (1826–90), creator of Pinocchio (Mauri 1987, 16).

27. Mauri (1987, table 1.1).

28. The discussion of Italian publishing comes from Forgacs (1990a) and from Mauri (1987); the concentration percentages are from Mauri.

considerations. Most Italian newspapers are intensely regional. They are supported by local advertisers who aim for local market; they carry local news for local readers; and they face little serious competition within their regional markets. Difficulties of distribution owing to the length and mountains of the Italian peninsula were a major influence in the development of the newspapers serving regional markets, and while the distribution costs are less significant today, the regionalist press has become firmly established. (*La Repubblica* is the exceptional case in being a truly national newspaper.) Books, on the other hand, depend on sales alone, since they do not carry advertising. Any title must compete not only with other Italian works, but with foreign translations as well. And there is no equivalent to the press's reporting of local cultural events, sports results, or business transactions. Therefore the industrial logic of book publishing does not favor regionalism, while the industrial logic of newspaper publishing does.

Writing and producing books, moreover, is only one outlet for creativity. In Italy during the twentieth century, and especially during the postwar period, many writers saw their opportunities for artistic expression and social influence to lie in cinema, not in books. The prestige of films and filmmaking, especially during the crucial era from the 1940s to the 1970s, drew creative energies away from literature per se. In Italy, a progression from writer to filmmaker was a natural form for artistic success to take. This had impact not only on literature in general, but on budding regionalism in particular, because making movies, unlike making poetry or fiction, is highly capital intensive and therefore requires that the creator aim for a mass audience right from the beginning. Pier Paolo Pasolini provides a well-known example of someone who moved from regionalism to a more national-international voice as he moved from poetry to film. Beginning his literary career with poetry in the Friulian dialect (and, later, with novels about lower-class life in Rome that made use of Roman dialect), by the 1960s he had turned his creative energies to film. In addressing a mass audience and becoming himself a cultural object, Pasolini's regionalism faded.

Italy

Finally comes the peculiarly Italian factor, specifically, the question of the extent to which Italy represents a unified cultural system. It is often said that Italy presents the paradox of being highly centralized administratively, yet having a weak sense of unity and little nationalist sentiment. This common wisdom is open to dispute on the cultural front, however, in light of the overwhelming honor paid to Italy's classical and Renaissance heritage. There may or may not be an "Italy" but there is clearly an Italian culture, in which all Italians take both pride and (directly or indirectly) profit. Italians are aware of having a cultural stake in "Italy"—in Rome, in Florence, in Venice, in Dante, in Leonardo—more, perhaps, than they are aware of having a political or economic stake.

What would happen to this culture if Italy were to fragment into some more de-centered, federalist structure? The economic and political advantages of greater regional autonomy vary. For the South, since the elite has been co-opted into the central state government and since it remains a relatively poor area on the receiving end of cross-regional economic transfers, enthusiasm for separatism of any sort is understandably rare, since neither the economic nor the political elites have anything to gain. The situation is different in the North. Umberto Bossi and his Northern League movement that calls for loosening ties with Rome and points south has considerable appeal; and even those Northerners who dismiss Bossi like to point out that if Italy were divided in the middle, the North might be the wealthiest nation in Europe. Nevertheless, the cultural cost of such separation would be enormous, since the North would lose much of its claim to the classical and Renaissance heritage. It is one thing to lose the Roman bureaucracy, in other words; it is quite another thing to lose the Roman Colosseum.[29]

29. Although there is no current push for separatism in the Mezzogiorno, there was an active Sicilian separatist movement in the 1940s, supported by an unlikely combination of landowners, leftists, and the Mafia, and temporarily tolerated by the

While increased regional autonomy could work to encourage literary and cultural regionalism, one must also remember that "region" is a relational concept, in that places are always defined relative to other places. Italy exhibits what we might call the "no Paris" phenomenon: the absence of a single center for cultural production. In literature and the arts there are multiple centers of activity in Italy—Milan for publishing and design, Rome for broadcasting, Naples for popular music—but no one metropolis toward which all aspiring creative intellectuals are drawn. This lack of a single cultural center like Paris or New York City has a paradoxical result in preventing the construction of a periphery. Cultural regionalism is first and foremost an assertion of otherness. In Italy there is no single place, no cultural center against which "other" places define themselves.[30]

Furthermore, the Italian state is not a significant source of funding for literature. While the state supports the preservation and promotion of the cultural heritage—museums, libraries, infrastructure (the name of the ministry "di turismo e della spettacolo" is telling)—there is almost no support for writers or literary activities. State support for literature, funneled through regional administrative units, has the paradoxical impact of encouraging literary regionalism, as we shall see in the following chapter. In Italy, what little support there is for writers (for example, for theatrical writing) comes from the local levels of government. So there is no cultural federalism, no desire to balance the needs of different regions, no political trade-offs of the sort that seem to encourage regional distinctiveness in other places.

Cultural centers encourage cultural expression on the periphery. A culturally dominant metropolis can provoke the articulation of existing regional identities through contrast and in

---

Allies. It faded away once Sicily was given autonomous status in 1945. See Finkelstein (1998).

30. See Asor Rosa (1989) on the contradictory pressures toward *centralismo* and *policentrismo*. Dainotto (2000) argues that literary nationalism and regionalism are not opposites, but are two discursive formations of the same impulse toward a cultural, often ethnic, purity.

resistance. In addition, centrally collected but locally distributed funding can enhance existing collective identities through resources. In Italy the situation is the opposite. Both the absence of an acknowledged cultural center and the lack of central support funneled to the peripheries act to discourage regional cultural expressions, regardless of the strength of the pre-existing regional identities.

To sum up, a variety of factors—the lack of a single cultural center, late literacy development, the economics of publishing, the universal ideologies of intellectuals in general and the cosmopolitanism of the literary elite in particular—all work against the development of regional literary cultures in Italy. Despite their personal local affinities, neither writers nor publishers nor readers find it in their interests to organize their literary practices along regional lines. This is why although Italians hold regionalism as an emotional attachment and produce individual regionalist writers, the Italian culture does not give rise to literature as a cultural movement or frame.

Members of Italy's reading class are literary cosmopolitans. The old image of cosmopolitan versus local is misleading, however, for these are not all-or-nothing categorizations. Cosmopolitans can select cultural objects like they do any other consumer good. Specifically, Italian cosmopolitans, whether or not they are cowbirds who have moved from one region to another, can pick and choose their localisms. They express their local affinities through preferences in food, but not in literature. This selectivity is from the consumption side, but the same capacity for selection is true of cultural producers, such as literary elites. Given the resources, intellectuals can articulate collective identity and promote its institutionalization. As a rule, they will only do this when such regionalism does not compromise their political convictions or career interests. In Italy, it rarely pays for literary elites to produce or consume place.[31]

---

31. There are relatively few Italian cowbirds, for in recent years Italy has not had a great deal of residential mobility. "The overall level of internal mobility in Italy is today

When artists and intellectuals do not play a leadership role, it is popular culture, not literature, that is the vehicle for regional collective identity. Italian popular regionalism expresses itself through cuisine, folk music, dialect, dress, and even—to the dismay of Italian cosmopolitans—the regionalist political parties. Markets, for tourists or for votes, can play a strong role here. Thus Italy reproduces its paradoxical situation of having intense popular regionalism and a surprising absence of literary regionalism.

---

very low in comparison to past experience and the situation in other countries . . . High homeownership rates, high indirect costs of moving and past emigration might be some of the factors contributing to relative low interregional mobility today" (Bonifazi et al. 2005).

State Patronage in Norway and the U.S.

WITH FREDRIK ENGELSTAD[1]

Literary regionalism occurs when the reading class favors writers from or literary works about a particular region. Under these conditions, a place-based resonance occurs between the literature and the readers. Nothing about the resonance or about the availability of literary regionalism is automatic, however. Institutional conditions must be favorable, as we saw in the case of Italy, where they were not. Yet institutional conditions are necessary but not sufficient. This chapter will show that literary regionalism flourishes only where there are both regional collective identity and institutional support.

Explanations of regionalism come in two standard forms. The first emphasizes *common experience*. People occupy a particular

1. This chapter is a shortened version of Griswold and Engelstad (1998). Most of the data are from the mid-1990s. Since then there have been no major changes in either the State funding or the patterns of literary regionalism that are described here. Note that in order to avoid confusion, this chapter uses the convention of referring to American states with a lowercase *s* and to "the state" in the sense of central administration with a capital *S*.

place with particular natural resources and challenges, the theory goes, and over time they maintain their community through economic activities and associated practices, traditions, and worldviews. Regionalism is always present in a culture because it rests on the bedrock of a unique package of historical experience. This experiential view is both the commonsense understanding of where regionalism comes from and the one found in the introduction to virtually every anthology of regional writing. The second explanation, favored by sociologists, downplays the role of history in favor of *institutional supports.* While regional sentiments, a local sense of place, may always be present, in and of themselves they are latent. Only an infusion of new resources allows such sentiments to reach an effective level of cultural articulation. In this view, a region is more a social creation than natural cultural formation.

This chapter attempts to sort out the claims of the experiential and institutionalist views by asking, can resource flows in and of themselves create and sustain regionalism? The empirical focus is on Norway and the United States, both of which experienced a dramatic increase in State literary support in the mid-1960s. These two developments are totally independent of each other—it is a coincidence that they both occurred the same year—and they allow the examination of several decades of State literary patronage in two different national contexts. So the question is: what difference has State patronage made for literary regionalism?"

State Support and Regional Literature

Regionalism is a form of collective identity. Over and above aesthetic content, it takes the form of either a cultural movement or a cultural frame. A regionalist *movement* is intentionally initiated by the producers of literature, for example the writers from a particular area who organize to promote their common interests, while a *frame* is imposed from outside, for example by an editor putting together an anthology of writers from the Great Plains. The relationship between movement and frame is often dialectical and some of the key players occupy a middle ground—a regional publisher and promoter of local poetry is both producing and framing—but as ideal types there is a distinction between internally-generated movements and externally-imposed frames. Collective identity may (or may not, as in the Italian case) give rise to a regionalist literary movement, and it may or may not be encouraged by a regionalist literary frame.[2]

Alberto Melucci, one of the initiators of the "new social movements" scholarship, has argued that collective identity is not a given, but something that needs to be explained. Its achievement is an ongoing process:

> *Collective identity is an interactive and shared definition produced by several interacting individuals who are concerned with the orientations of their action as well as the field of opportunities and constraints in which their action takes place.* The process of constructing, maintaining, and altering a collective identity provides the basis for actors to shape their expectations and calculate the costs and benefits of their action. Collective identity formation is a delicate process and requires continual investments. As it comes to resemble more institutionalized forms of social action, collective identity may crystallize into organizational forms . . . In less institutionalized forms of action its character more closely resembles a process which must be continually activated in order for action to be possible.

Crystallized or in process, collective identity in Melucci's view has three dimensions: the *cognitive* (a shared definition of means and ends, a common sense of what is at stake), the *relational* (networks of interaction and communication), and the *emotional* (the investment of feelings, affective meanings over and above

2. A cultural movement is a form of collective action whereby agents intend to effect a change in the symbolic domain. A cultural movement may generate or be derived from a social movement, but the two are analytically distinct; cultural movements aim at influencing symbolic expression, while social movements aim at influencing social policy.

rational calculations). An input on any of the three dimensions can intensify collective identity.[3] State literary patronage most directly affects the relational dimension. While people may share a cognitive and emotional identification with a region, putting them in contact with one another (e.g., through technologies that enhance communication, or through conferences that bring far-flung writers together) may produce a recognized collective identity, which then may lead to further collective literary activities. State funding of conferences, festivals, writers' workshops, even the dissemination of knowledge about how to obtain the patronage itself, enhances these relations.

So, paradoxically, central State literary patronage encourages regionalism. It does so in three ways: First, State patronage frees writers from the need to live in the metropolitan center or to cater to non-local audiences. Second, if resources are distributed through regional organizations, groups attempting to win these resources will organize themselves along regional lines. Third, such patronage cultivates Melucci's relational dimension of collective identity.

When writers depend on markets, as they have ever since the decline of aristocratic patronage, they typically move toward institutional centers, as in the familiar gravitation of talent toward Rome, London, Paris, or New York. Two types of opportunities await them. The first is commercial: writers aiming for a wide readership seek to broaden their experience, to avoid provincialism, and to be known to a national audience. The second is institutional: writers seek publishers, libraries, bookstores, literary journals, intellectual networks, and contact with the reading class, all of which cluster in large cities.

State patronage reduces both types of centripetal pull. To the extent that it relieves writers' total dependence on the market, it allows them to set aside purely commercial concerns in favor of aesthetic or political ones, either of which may inspire regionalist

---

3. Melucci (1989); quotation from 34–35 (italics in original).

writing. State support makes it possible for more people in more places either to earn a living as authors or at least to legitimate their claims to being writers. In addition, government support often fosters institutions operating at the regional level, such as local publishers, writers' cooperatives, book fairs, writers' workshops, and author lectures. These make the intellectual attractions of the metropolis less compelling and contribute to relational networks.

State resources are often distributed on a regional basis, and this further enhances local relationships. To take a Norwegian example, the State-funded Authors Center in Kristiansand brings together writers and the reading class of southern Norway. Such regional relationships encourage institutional isomorphism, as authors and promoters of literature organize their activities on a regional level as well. In the U.S., the National Endowments for the Arts and for the Humanities distribute a significant percentage of endowment funds to the individual states. This decentralized budgetary authority mandated the establishment of state-level arts councils, which are public agencies, and humanities councils, which are private and largely volunteer. While there is some overlap, the arts councils sponsor creative work and training, while the humanities councils sponsor events drawing on history, literature, and the arts. The programs of these councils foster communication and identification at the regional (in this case, state) level. The federal government (NEA/NEH) and state councils, therefore, provide regionalist input to Melucci's relational dimension, and when the programs are successful, to the cognitive and emotional dimensions as well.[4]

The question is, can such institutional inputs of resources establish a regional collective identity, or must some such identity exist first? To answer this, we will examine four regions in two very different literary systems, both of which experiences a boost in State support in the late 1960s.

It is a coincidence that State support increased in Norway and the United States at the same time. There was no mutual influence between the two on the matter. The differences between the

---

4. See Hagen (1996, 44–50) for a discussion of the Kristiansand Authors Center.

two countries being vast, the following discussion does not make a direct Norwegian-American comparison. At the same time, the very differences between the two systems of support make the internal comparisons—between regions within Norway, between states within the U.S.—illuminating.

The essential difference between the literary worlds of Norway and the U.S. is the difference between a welfare state and a market. Norway's welfare state has been one of the most all-encompassing in western Europe. Oil revenues plus a small population have allowed the State to provide generous social supports, and while literature is a tiny part of this, its funding is lavish. Norway, as a matter of State policy, treats its writers better than any country on earth.

Although the United States does not treat its writers especially poorly—they are rarely hung, imprisoned, or censored—it by and large leaves them to sink or swim in the market. A few popular authors get fabulously wealthy, while most earn little or nothing. A bit of State funding comes through NEA and NEH programs, though this is short term (and in the case of the NEH doesn't go to individual writers anyway). Indirect federal support comes via private nonprofit foundations and through universities, though few writers can count on these. In comparison with Norway, government support for literature is meager.

This difference allows one to look at the relationship between State supports and literary regionalism in a system that has largely freed writers from the market and one that has not done so. Comparing two regions within each country reveals how State support's impact on regional literature varies even within the same context. In Norway, the two regions are the West Coast and the Far North; in the U.S., the regions are Maine and Illinois. The internal comparisons hold constant the differences in context—market versus welfare state—and allow one to discern the conditions under which a common infusion of resources, lavish or meager, can give rise to a regionalist literary identity. Indicators that register literary regionalism include reading patterns, anthologies, the organization of bookstores and libraries, and college courses.

State Patronage and Regionalism in Norway

Ruled by Denmark until 1814 and in political union with Sweden until 1905, Norway did not develop a national literature until the mid-nineteenth century. In the 1850s National Romanticism, an intellectual movement drawing on a growing literary market, aimed to integrate folklore and regional elements into a distinctly Norwegian literature.[5]

One focus of the movement was language itself. Although Danish had remained Norway's official language after 1814, by midcentury reformers were working on aligning the written language with the Norwegian spoken by the educated public of Oslo. National Romanticist intellectuals protested bitterly. They developed an alternative linguistic strategy based on a Nynorsk ("New Norwegian") language constructed from West Coast and inland rural dialects, which they maintained derived from the Old Norse of the medieval Sagas. They wanted Nynorsk, not what they scorned as "Dano-Norwegian," to be the official Norwegian language. The movement achieved partial success—Nynorsk became Norway's second official language in 1885 and was used by some prominent writers like Arne Garborg in the late nineteenth century and Olav Dunn in the early twentieth—but the dream of national hegemony never came to pass, and Nynorsk remains a minority language.[6]

Nynorsk was one of a cluster of late nineteenth century countercultural movements based in western and southwestern Norway (temperance and Pietism were two others) that Stein Rokkan called the "revolt of the periphery." These movements firmly established the claims and rights of regions outside the capital. Though the content has changed (though not entirely, for

---

5. Examples include: Bjørnstjerne Bjørnson's *Peasant Tales* from the West Coast; A. O. Vinje's poems from the Southeast; Henrik Ibsen's *Peer Gynt* from the inner East; Jonas Lie's tales from the North; and Amalie Skram's Bergen tetralogy, *People from the Helle Marsh*.

6. Nynorsk is used by a majority in rural parts of the West Coast and the inner West. Some 10 percent of Norwegians use Nynorsk regularly, and 17 percent of students in primary schools use Nynorsk. Users of Nynorsk and Bokmål (standard Norwegian) have no difficulty understanding one another. Statistics Norway (1996b, table 143).

proponents of Nynorsk are still passionate), regional cleavages have been remarkably stable and influential in Norwegian politics.[7]

Regional cleavage characterizes literary institutions as well. Oslo is the home of all the major publishing houses (including those specializing in Nynorsk literature) as well as the most influential newspapers and literary journals. Publishing initiatives outside the city are usually short lived. Some half of the members of the Norwegian Authors' Union live in or near Oslo, as opposed to about one-fifth of the population as a whole. (The Authors' Union, both trade union and guild, restricts membership to those who have published at least two books.) Outside of the Oslo area, the West Coast and the North have the most Authors' Union members. A number of regional and subregional authors' unions, with more liberal membership criteria, attract younger, less established writers, thus fostering regional relationships and identification early in their careers.[8]

State support of literature rests on three pillars: the Purchasing Scheme, the income warranty for artists, and the exemption from sales tax that books enjoy. Under the Purchasing Scheme, the Council of Cultural Affairs buys 1000 copies of every work of fiction written in Norwegian and distributes them to public libraries. Under the income warranty, any recognized author receives a minimal income of 120,000 Norwegian kroner (roughly $19,000) per year. In addition, members of the national Authors' Union can compete for stipends distributed by the Union's Literary Council; a quarter or more of the Union members get these annually. Under the sales tax provision, books are exempt

7. See Rokkan (1970). A recent example of regional political clout came in the form of the successful campaign against Norway joining the European Union in 1972 and in 1994. Norwegians from the Oslo area and the center of the country tended to favor membership, while those from the West and Southwest opposed it.

8. Hagen (1996, 42–43). If we take the Oslo area to be two counties—Oslo and Akershus—then in 1991, the census year closest to the data collected here, the population of the two counties was 20.1% of the Norwegian population; 47% of the Authors' Union members lived in these two counties. If we use the more expansive definition of the Oslo region to include Østfold and Vestfold as well, we find the area accounts for 31% of the population and 53% of the Authors' Union membership. The population statistics come from Statistics Norway (2004, table 49).

from the high (23 percent) sales tax, making them relatively inexpensive in comparison to other consumer goods.

A fourth element, the public funding of the Norwegian Authors' Center (Norsk forfattersenter), is more modest financially, but critically important for regional literature. The Center, with its main office in Oslo and regional offices in Bergen, Kristiansand, Trondheim, and Tromsø, organizes author visits to schools, libraries, festivals, and other events in which the authors give readings and discuss their work. While the regional centers need not favor authors from their own areas, hosting institutions often express a preference for local writers. Because the Center is less restrictive than the national Authors' Union, younger, not-yet-established writers can join and get a chance to showcase their work. This structure, which parallels that of the Authors' Union, has the effect of dividing authors not only in terms of their residence, but also in terms of their affiliations; there is a national elite belonging to the Authors' Union and often living in Oslo, and there are local authors connected to regional centers and unions, and often living there as well.[9]

How does this system of State support affect readers? Since the 1000 books purchased by the State are distributed among some 1400 libraries, every library has most (though not all) works of Norwegian fiction. Moreover, the trade agreement between publishers and booksellers gives the members of the Association of Bookstores a monopoly on the sale of books and prohibits price competition; bookstores are obliged to keep all titles in stock for two years. The effect of this agreement is that the 424 Norwegian bookstores make quality literature readily available in all parts of the country.

Figures for actual reading behavior show little regional variation in terms of how much Norwegians read. Both the wide dispersion of bookstores and libraries and the minimal differences in education levels among the regions contribute to this

---

9. Events organized by the Authors' Centers are funded jointly by the Center and the hosting institution (school, library, etc.).

uniformity. Norwegians everywhere read, and they read a lot; Norway has one of the world's highest reading rates.[10] Does the Norwegian level of State patronage, the highest in the world, encourage regionalism? It should, because the support (1) allows writers to live in peripheral regions, (2) encourages writers' organizations and activities at the regional level, and (3) enriches networks of communication and support within a local literary world. While it is plausible that the post-1965 State literary support was a boon to the literary expression of regional collective identity, it would not explain variations in outcomes. Some regional literary cultures seem more robust than others, and even-handed State funding cannot account for this. To understand this type of variation requires internal comparison. Norwegians regard the West Coast and North Norway as having especially distinctive characters, so they offer appropriate cases for consideration.[11]

The four counties of the West Coast have a population of slightly more than one million people, and have two major cities, Bergen and Stavanger. Bergen, Norway's largest city for many years, has been a shipping center exporting fish from the north to the continent since the Middle Ages. While Stavanger also based its early economy on fish, today it is the center for North Sea oil drilling; indeed the petroleum industry's imprint is felt throughout the West Coast.[12]

10. Eighty percent of Norwegian adults report having read a book during the previous year, and 40 percent have visited a public library. Statistics Norway (1996a, table 47). See also Hagen (1996, 69–73).

11. See Øidne (1959) for the classic discussion. While there is some disagreement about regional boundaries, political scientist Stein Rokkan identified six political regions of Norway, each with a distinct political and demographic profile, and these correspond to most Norwegians' conceptions of cultural regions as well. The six are: Oslofjord region (Oslo, Akershus, Østfold, Vestfold); the Inner East (Hedmark, Oppland, Buskerud, Telemark); the South (Aust-Agder, Vest-Agder); the West Coast (Rogaland, Hordaland, Sogn og Fjordane, More og Romsdal); Middle Norway (Sør-Trøndelag, Nord-Trøndelag); and the North (Nordland, Troms, Finnmark). Henrichsen and Rokkan (1977).

12. The four counties of the West Coast had a population of 1,093,820 in 1991, 26% of the country as a whole. By 2004, the population had grown slightly, to 1,185,699, and was still 26% of the total. Statistics Norway (2004, table 49).

FIGURE 9. Map of Norway's counties and regions

The three counties of the North have only half the population of the West Coast. Though largely north of the Arctic
Circle, the Gulf Stream creates a relatively mild climate, making
agriculture possible farther north here than anywhere else in the
world; *The Growth of the Soil,* Nobel laureate Knut Hamsun's
homage to the farmer-settler, is set in the middle of Troms at
seventy degrees latitude. The traditional Northern way of life
depends on the rich fisheries off the coast, along with small-scale
farming. Tromsø is the main commercial center.[13]

13. The North had 460,809 people in 1991 (11% of the total). In 2004, it had 462,895
(10% of the total). Statistics Norway (2004, table 49).

Both the West Coast and the North feature a stark landscape and long, rugged coastline. Both regions are rural; half of the population of the North and more than 40 percent in the West live outside of towns having more than 2000 people. The North is the least densely populated region in the country, with only 5 people per square kilometer; the West has some 25, although with significant variation among counties, from 42 in Rogaland to 6 in Sogn og Fjordane.[14]

While most of Norway is ethnically homogeneous, one exception is the significant Sami minority in the North, especially in Finmark. Sami language, entirely different from Norwegian, has official status and there exists a small Sami-language literature. Norway has seen a modest influx of non-European immigrants in recent decades, but these have had little impact on literary life.

The expansion of the national university system beginning in the late 1960s constituted the University of Bergen as a major academic center and established a new university at Tromsø. The movement for mass higher education also led to the development of regional colleges throughout the country, which has contributed to an equalization of educational attainment. About 20 percent of Norwegians have attained higher education. There is some regional variation—not surprisingly, the Oslo area has the most highly educated people, the West Coast roughly the national average, the North below average—but the differences are not dramatic. Similarly, the income differences between regions are slight, although both the North and the West Coast are somewhat below the national average. The occupational structures of the two regions are similar, with less than 10 percent in either still working in agriculture and fisheries.[15]

---

14. Statistics Norway (1996b, tables 33 and 34). Cf. Statistics Norway (2005, tables 47 and 48).

15. The education figures come from Statistics Norway (1996b, table 136). The percent of all Norwegians having higher education is 19.5%. In Oslo, it is 31.5%, but Oslo and Akershus are exceptional. The rest of the country has about 20% higher education in more urban counties, somewhat less in more rural ones. In Hordaland, in the West, which includes the city of Bergen, 20.6% of adults have higher education,

Since education and income are correlated with reading, these regional similarities suggest little significant difference between the reading cultures of the North and the West Coast. The West Coast, because of its considerably larger and somewhat more urban population, does have more large newspapers. Data on book reading and on loans of books from public libraries suggest that readers from both regions have similar reading practices and are close to the national average.[16]

Given that the West Coast and the North share characteristics of being peripheral areas of a highly centralized country, and given their rough equality in terms of education and reading, one would anticipate that the infusion of State literary support would have similar results in both, namely, an upturn in literary regionalism. A closer look at the two areas reveals unanticipated differences.

Starting with the West Coast, one must first take account of the lasting impact of Nynorsk. Autodidact linguist Ivar Aasen started collecting samples of Norwegian vernacular in the 1840s, sowing the seeds of what would become the Nynorsk movement. For many years however, few writers of serious literature used it; even on the West Coast, the emerging modern literature was in Bokmål, which used standard Norwegian. In the 1880s, Arne Garborg, who grew up near Stavanger, emerged as the leading advocate of the Nynorsk movement. Writers inspired by Garborg began producing a regionally oriented literature in Nynorsk, which flourished through the 1930s and continues to the present. In addition to Nynorsk, West Coast regionalism includes a self-assertive Bergen literature, which developed from the 1970s, partly as a result of the university's expansion.

The West Coast has both the personnel and institutions to encourage literary regionalism. Fifteen percent of the national Authors' Union members live there. Moreover, prolific Nynorsk writers who reside in Oslo retain strong ties to the region. West Coast authors win more than their share of literary prizes and of

---

while in the three Northern counties the figure is about 16%. Cf. Statistics Norway (2005, table 180). The income figures are from Statistics Norway (1993).

16. Statistics Norway (1996b, table 221); Statistics Norway (1996a, table 47).

critical studies. As for institutional supports, the Bergen Authors' Center, organizational heart of West Coast literary life, concentrates on the central West and, recently, the southwest. As a result of the Center's strength, no regional Authors' Union has been necessary, though two local authors' unions in Sogn og Fjordane and Møre og Romsdal assist novice writers. Literary and cultural festivals, which celebrate collective identity, abound. In the annual Arts Festival in Bergen, under the auspices of the West Coast Authors' Center, writers from the region and elsewhere in Norway give readings. Stavanger's annual Kapittel literary festival originated as a celebration of local literature and recently has widened its scope; similarly the Bjørnson festival in Molde both honors the city's greatest son and celebrates national and international authors.[17]

So with all these institutional supports and all these committed writers, and given lavish State patronage, is West Coast literary regionalism indeed flourishing? An examination of the specific indicators of literary collective identity revealed the following:

1. Anthologies and journals. The West Coast lacks both specifically local anthologies and a successful regional literary magazine. Norway had thirty-seven regional literary anthologies published between 1980 and the late 1990s, but only three featured West Coast authors, and even these did not cover the entire region, but only small parts.[18]

2. Reader preferences. The picture is mixed. There is a general tendency for Norwegian readers to prefer books from their own region. When asked to name their favorite authors, however, people from the West Coast show a lower propensity than the national average to name a West Coast author. On the other hand, data from book club members suggests that West Coast readers favor regional authors for contemporary fiction.[19]

3. University courses. Literature courses linked to the region appear only sporadically at the University of Bergen and no-

17. The information on prizes and studies comes from Hagen (1996, 160ff); the discussion of the Bergen Authors' Center's activities comes from Hagen (1996, 122ff).

18. See Hagen (1996, 80). There was a county-based literary magazine, *Sogn og Fjordane Magasin,* that lasted for seven years in the 1980s.

19. Hagen 1996.

where else. One (paradoxical) influence is the requirement that Nynorsk literature be taught as part of the general canon to avoid stigmatizing it as parochial, so the regional language strenuously denies its regional nature. The Hordaland Academy of Writing offers annual courses to students hoping to start a writing career, but it does not function on a regional basis and draws students from the entire country.

In sum, we do not find a robust West Coast literary identity. It may be that sensitivity to place is less important in this region, or it may be that subregional units loom larger in people's collective identity. Bergen, for example, has a centuries-old urban culture, and books with a distinct Bergen setting sell an extra several thousand copies there. Library loans in Sunnhordland show similar localism. The region as a whole, however, does not seem to generate much literary identification.[20]

Northern Norway is a different story altogether. Writers have celebrated its dramatic landscape, extremes of daylight and darkness, and harsh living conditions for centuries. The eighteenth century minister Petter Dass, considered the first modern Norwegian author, devoted his writing to the region, and later writers, above all Knut Hamsun, have celebrated the North. Only recently, however, has a regional literary movement emerged.

Because of its small and scattered population, the North does not have as elaborate a cultural infrastructure as the one found on the West Coast—it does not have newspapers with national standing or major repertory theatres, for example—but its literary world has some institutional supports. One is the Northern Norwegian Council for Cultural Affairs, funded by municipal and county budgets, which distributes funds to bolster the cultural life of the region. The city of Tromsø and its university attract sufficient intellectual resources to constitute a viable literary milieu, and half of the North's national Authors' Union members live there. Tromsø is also home to the Northern Norwegian Authors' Union (Nordnorsk forfatterlag, or NNFL), the leading organi-

20. The library-loans finding comes from Henmoe (1996).

zational force for regional literature; many NNFL members do not belong to the national Authors' Union, so their literary affiliation is strictly local. The NNFL gathers writers for seminars, sponsors regional anthologies, and publishes a journal. When the NNFL was established in 1972, only a handful of books by North authors were published; five years later, publishers, many local, were bringing out sixty titles a year.

The annual Northern Norway Festival in Harstad, a showcase for regional music and the arts, attracts authors from all over the North for readings and discussions. An annual "Day of the Book" circulates among cities of the North. Hamsun Days celebrates the region's most prominent writer, who grew up in the Vesterålen archipelago and set most of his novels in the North.

What of regional literature in the North? With these modest but robust institutions, and with the infusion of State patronage since the mid-1960s, regionalism emerges as follows:

1. Anthologies and journals. A viable regional literary magazine, *Nordnorsk magasin,* has been published regularly since 1979. A second journal called *Skarven,* put out by the NNFL, includes both fiction and literary criticism. As for anthologies, twelve of the thirty-seven regional anthologies that appeared in the 1980s and 1990s featured North writers exclusively.

2. Reader preferences. The public in the North shows a stronger preference for their regional authors than readers from other regions or the national average. Thus holds true both when northern Norwegians are asked to name their favorite author and when book club members make their monthly selections.[21]

3. University courses. The University of Tromsø regularly offers courses on North Norwegian literature. Moreover, courses in creative writing are organized on a regular basis, and in contrast to similar courses in the West, they are explicitly directed toward writers and potential writers from the region.

In short, literary regionalism thrives in the North. Funding sources, organizational activities, local publishing, reader prefer-

21. See Hagen (1996, 64).

ences, and education all show clear and multiple indications of a regional collective literary identity.

So why are the West and the North so different? One line of speculation involves critical mass of literary activities. The Purchasing Scheme and an associated bundle of literary supports led to a substantial increase in both the number of books published and the number of people actively pursuing a writing career. If the Purchasing Scheme led to a doubling of the number of authors, which seems a conservative estimate, Hagen has calculated that without the Scheme the West Coast would have had thirty-three authors by the 1990s, and the North only sixteen. And while it is difficult to say what constitutes a critical mass for a local literary system, sixteen seems below the limit. So the sheer numeric impact of the Purchasing Scheme may have been more critical in the North for forming a regional literary identity.[22]

Beyond this, we note striking differences between the West Coast and the North: Even if the West has more recognized authors, the traces of regional collective identity are much less visible. Regionalism in the West centers on smaller geographical units like the district of Sunnhordland, the county of Sogn og Fjordane, or the city of Bergen. In the North, literary activities embrace the entire region. The aims of organizations, funding sources, and festival organizers are regional as well; their goal is to enhance North Norwegian writing, not a literature associated with Tromsø or Lofoten.

How is this to be explained? Differences in regional orientation originate from a set of causes deeper than the contingencies of organizational structure, including a mix of demographic and geographical factors. For instance, it seems likely that thin populations are especially self-aware. Beyond density, history and timing influence the formation of regional identities. Collective identity on the West Coast arose in the last half of the nineteenth century and took the form of the Nynorsk movement, which had aimed well beyond the West. The Nynorsk movement defied

22. The numbers here refer to Hagen (1996, table 3.2).

the established, Oslo-centered high culture and claimed to represent the true Norwegian cultural heritage. The result was that energies that might have gone into regional endeavors were devoted to national goals. Thus, paradoxically, movements for a specifically West Coast identity have been weak. The cultural ambitions of the West today are very high—as manifested in the press, theaters, musical life, festivals, etc.—but the intent is to constitute a "second center," a part of the cultural landscape on an equal basis with Oslo, not to further regional specificity.

The cultural self-consciousness of the North, on the other hand, came into articulation during a mid-1960s political shift toward greater decentralization. This reorganization involved setting up regional development organizations, and it happened to concur with the introduction of the national literary support systems. This happy combination encouraged cultural entrepreneurs in the North to exploit State patronage for regional purposes and apply literary and cultural support systems at a regional level.

Moreover, differences in the scope of the two regions' cultural ambitions were dramatic. In contrast to the West, the aims of the North were always focused on the region itself. Northerners were concerned with protecting their own resources and way of life, not creating a basis for political or cultural dominance. Thus the North's regional literary identity was to some extent a product of having a modest and highly local agenda, while the West's tepid regionalism was a product of its more exalted aspirations.

State Patronage and Regionalism in the United States

Among many differences between Norway and the United States, two seem especially germane to regionalism. The first is that in the United States, market mechanisms rule. Despite the increased State support since the mid-1960s, and despite occasional university or private foundational grants, most American writers and literary organizations must depend on a readership willing to buy their works. The U.S. has nothing like the web of support that Norway offers. The second difference is that Norway's State activities are highly centralized, whereas under America's federal system, considerable political and institutional power devolves to states and localities. To illustrate how sharp the contrast with Norway is, recently many Norwegians have called for abolishing the counties altogether, for since they no longer run the hospitals, they are seen as a rather meaningless level of government. A similar movement in the United States—abolish Ohio?—is unthinkable.[23]

The United States, like Norway, developed its modern literature in an atmosphere of defensive nationalism. Sharing the anxiety of the periphery, both nations denied their inferiority to some cultural center—the center being Copenhagen or continental Europe for Norwegian writers, London or Europe for Americans—by inflecting nineteenth-century Romanticism into a celebration of their particular natural and social landscapes.

Both landscapes varied more sharply in the U.S. Long before the Civil War, distinctive New England and Southern literatures had developed, and the postbellum local-color movement celebrated America's multiple regions. The Southern Renaissance of the 1920s and 1930s and the Federal Writers' Project codification of state and regional cultures carried on the place-specific tradition. Thus almost from the beginning, the conception of a specifically American literature coincided with regionalism. In the context of American federalism, where powers not constitutionally allocated to the central government devolve to the states and where "states' rights" have been asserted to the point of secession, expressions of localism and regionalism are seen as very American. Americans have consistently maintained the idea of being nationalist by being local.

American writers are not immune to the lure of the city, but they are drawn to more than one. Authors cluster on both coasts

23. Only about 10% of the financing for nonprofit arts organizations in the U.S. comes from public funds, and most of this is local (6%), while another 2% comes from the state and 2% from the federal government. Individuals (20%), foundations (13%), and corporations (7%), along with the public financing, contribute half of arts financing; the other half comes from earned income in such forms as ticket sales and subscriptions (National Endowment for the Arts 2004b, 2).

and in university towns. In terms of sheer numbers, California, New York, and Illinois have the most writers, with New York having the highest concentration of authors in the labor force. Rural inland states like Wyoming and North Dakota have the fewest writers. American authors are even more urban than the rest of the population. Although authors may write from everywhere, publishers cluster in New York.[24]

Readers are everywhere. Book readers are more common on the West Coast and in the northeast, especially New England, but in all regions close to half of the adult population read books. Reading rates are higher in the suburbs and in central cities than in rural areas, and education, as always, is the best predictor of reading.[25]

So the United States has a readership that is decentralized, a publishing industry that is centralized, writers who live in urban centers all over, and a strong tradition of regional cultural identity. Now what happens when you add State support?

In the mid-1960s, the State got directly involved in supporting literature and the arts for the first time since the New Deal. In the early years of his administration Lyndon Johnson extended the reach of the State into new areas, including culture. An act of 1965 set up the National Endowment for the Arts and the National Endowment for the Humanities as independent grant-making agencies to free the arts and humanities from total market dependence. The endowments serve different purposes: the NEA supports creative work, performance, and training in the arts, while the NEH, with a slightly larger budget, supports research and humanities education and seeks to "foster in the

24. Ninety percent of American authors, as opposed to 80 percent of the population as a whole, live in metropolitan areas (Ellis and Beresford 1994, table 14). State author data comes from Ellis and Beresford (1994, table 5).

25. The data on readers come from National Endowment for the Arts (2004a, ch. 3). The study finds the suburban literary reading rate to be 49%, the central-city rate to be 47%, and the rural reading rate to be 41% (13). See also National Endowment for the Arts (1998, 51, table 30) for data on reading that distinguish New England from the rest of the northeast; the New England rate of reading literature is 69.7% while the mid-Atlantic is 63.3%. As in the later study, the West Coast is high (66.9%) and the Midwest and South somewhat lower, roughly 61%.

American people a greater curiosity about and understanding of the humanities." Both the NEA and the NEH support literary activities, but literature is central to the latter, so this discussion will concentrate there.[26]

While some NEH funding—research fellowships, preservation projects—are centrally funded, others are funded at the state level. The NEH supports humanities councils in every state and territory, and these councils set their own grant guidelines and award grants to programs within the state. The programs are geared for a non-specialist audience. If there were a connection between central (State) support and regional (state) culture, then the state humanities councils—which both depend upon and promote a cultural sensibility at the state level—would be a key link.

To see how this works out in practice, we turn to two very different states: Maine and Illinois. Maine is small, rural, and ethnically homogeneous, while Illinois is large, urban, and heterogeneous. Industrialization and the dramatic growth of Chicago drew European immigrants in the nineteenth century, followed by African Americans from the South, Mexicans, and Asians. Today the Chicago metropolitan area includes half of Illinois's population, and despite considerable inner-city poverty, people living in the Chicago CMSA (consolidated metropolitan statistical area, a U.S. Census term for metropolitan areas of over one million people) have higher incomes than the rest of the state. Not surprisingly, a political faulty line separates Chicago from downstate. It is only a slight exaggeration to say that legislators from outside the Chicago area, often Republicans, regard the city as a financial sinkhole and a nest of urban pathologies, while Chicago politicians, almost invariably Democrats, see their downstate counterparts as tightfisted hicks.[27]

---

26. In 2004, the budget for the National Endowment for the Humanities was $135 million, and the budget for the National Endowment for the Arts was $121 million (National Endowment for the Arts 2004b, 8).

27. Unless indicated otherwise, the percentages and figures on Maine and Illinois come from the U.S. Bureau of the Census (1996). In the mid-nineties Illinois was the

During the same period of rampant growth in Illinois, and as part of the same process, Maine and the rest of northern New England lost population as "the first agricultural region to grow old." Northern New England's decline, which began in the mid-nineteenth century, came about because of better soil in the opening West (including Illinois). Maine has always had a sharp sense of its distinctiveness. Such localism came from the state's history as the Massachusetts backwater, the New England state that didn't gain statehood until some thirty years after the rest of the East Coast. Its economy has depended on its forests—first for shipbuilding and then for paper—and on its dramatic coastline, which supports both tourism and fishing. Maine stayed rural as the rest of the country grew urban, stayed poor as the rest grew wealthier, stayed a "vacationland," a respite from real life. It has no large cities, is thinly populated, and is overwhelmingly white. Politically, Maine is fiercely independent—in 1992, maverick presidential candidate Ross Perot won 30.4 percent of Maine's votes, the highest in the nation; two-term governor Angus King was an independent; the state currently has two senators who are both moderate Republicans and women—and manifests a strong streak of libertarianism, unusual for an eastern state.[28]

Illinois is densely populated and urban. Maine is sparsely populated and rural. Illinois residents are also highly educated and affluent in comparison with Mainers.[29]

---

sixth largest state in the union, while Maine ranked thirty-ninth. By 2004 Census estimates, Illinois was fifth and Maine was fortieth (GCT-T1-R. Population Estimates (geographies ranked by estimate); Data Set: 2004 Population Estimates; Geographic Area: United States—State, and Puerto Rico). http://factfinder.census.gov/servlet/ GCTTable?_bm=y&-geo_id=D&-ds_name=D&-_lang=en&-redoLog=false&-format=ST-7S&-mt_name=PEP_2004_EST_GCTT1R_US9S&-CONTEXT=gct.

28. U. S. Census Bureau (1996, table 435). The classic discussion of the decline of northern New England is Wilson (1936); see also Barron (1984).

29. U. S. Census Bureau (1996, table 245). In Illinois, 13.6% of residents hold bachelor's degrees and 7.5% hold advanced degrees; in Maine, 12.7% hold bachelor's degrees and 6.1% hold advanced degrees. Thus Illinois is a little above the national average of 14.1% holding bachelor's degrees and 7.2% holding advanced degrees, and Maine is somewhat below. The income data is from table 699. In 2003, as in 1990 and

Since Illinoisans have higher average educations, higher incomes, and are less likely to live in the country, and since all of these are associated with reading, one might infer that people in Illinois read more than people in Maine. We have bits and pieces of evidence on this, though nothing conclusive. Newspaper circulation is about the same, .21 per capita in Illinois and .20 in Maine, though Illinois has ten times as many newspapers from which to chose. While Maine leads the nation in library books and serials per capita (Illinois is eighteenth), the two states are very close in actual circulation transactions per capita, which suggests that Mainers don't make especially high use of their well-stocked libraries. New England as a whole has higher reading rates than the Midwest does.[30]

The demographic and reading profiles suggest that the two states might have somewhat different reading cultures, with Illinois possibly being more robust because of its residents' greater education and urbanism. Given this background, when the NEH established the state humanities councils (the Illinois Humanities Council [IHC] was set up in 1973, the Maine Humanities Council [MHC] in 1975), what was the impact on regionalism? To answer this, we can take a look at each state's profile in the 1990s.

In Illinois, as in all states, a board of directors composed of people who are eminent in the humanities or who are socially prominent runs the Humanities Council. The board sets policy, initiates special projects, evaluates grant applications, and raises funds; a professional staff runs the daily operations. The IHC had a budget of around $1.4 million in the mid-1990s. About 80 percent of the budget went to programs, over half going to grants, the largest single expense item.[31]

The Illinois Humanities Council's mission statement begins: "Established on the premise that the humanities are central to any human enterprise involving serious decision or thought, the

30. Bowker (1996, 501) and National Endowment for the Arts (2004a, table 10).

31. Figures are from the Illinois Humanities Council Annual Report 1996: Overview.

IHC broadens public knowledge and appreciation of humanities throughout the state." A couple of things are striking here: first, the view that the humanities are tools for better decision-making, and second, the absence of any emphasis on works from or about Illinois. IHC-sponsored programs allow "the citizens of Illinois [to] learn about the human experience," and every annual report contains a map showing that funded projects are scattered throughout the state, but although the projects are *for* Illinoisans, they are not necessarily *about* Illinoisans.

Illinois Humanities Council grants are given to groups, not individuals, and for the vast majority of grants, the IHC support is only part, and usually a minor part, of the total funding. Projects are expected to raise "community support" from the local population or from foundation, corporate, and private benefactors. Indeed the IHC makes it very clear that the projects do not depend on government funding, but have private support. This is a very American style of "State support," one that downplays its own importance by presenting an image of local volunteerism and private philanthropy, with government just providing a helping hand.

How regional are the grants in content? Roughly 40 percent of the grants are primarily historical, and 20 percent or so are literary; other fields include music, cultural analysis, and contemporary affairs. During the period under observation, November 1994 to October 1996, the IHC awarded 115 grants, of which forty-eight (42 percent) were about Illinois or the Midwest: "Peoria Spirits" (an exhibit on the city's nineteenth-century distilling industry), "Freedom Train" (the Underground Railroad in Illinois), "An Evening of Stories by Illinois Authors," and so forth. The remaining sixty-seven grants went to projects like "The Quad City Mozart Festival."[32]

Intensive efforts have gone into promoting Illinois writers. In 1981, the Illinois State Library launched the "Read Illinois" program whose goal was to "significantly increase public awareness

32. This count comes from an untitled 16-page compilation from the Illinois Humanities Council (Griswold and Engelstad 1998).

and appreciation of Illinois' tremendous literary heritage." The
IHC supports various "Read Illinois" activities, such as an annual
conference on the Illinois Literary Heritage. One major product
of the collaboration was the 1985 publication of an impressive
volume called *A Reader's Guide to Illinois Literature.* Distributed
to libraries and schools throughout the state, the *Reader's Guide*
was and remains a superb resource.

Illinois has favorable demographics to support a reading culture, and the state's active and well-supported Humanities Council has done a good job of developing resources for and an appreciation of Illinois literature. All of this has been possible through
State-state patronage. So the question is, has it worked? Has this
application of money and energy succeeded in creating a collective sense of Illinois literature?

It seems not. The three indicators of literary regionalism suggest that the attempts to institutionalize the concept of Illinois
literature have not succeeded:

1. Anthologies and journals. Few anthologies are devoted to Illinois writers. Some exist—for example the IHC introduced
   Benchmark: An Anthology of Contemporary Illinois Poetry at a conference in 1988—but they are few and far between. Anthologies
   of Midwestern poets are more common, and anthologies of
   Chicago writers abound (e.g., *15 Chicago Poets* or the innumer-
   able anthologies of Chicago short stories). As for reviews, while
   there are a number of them, usually housed in university English departments and given some support from the Illinois Arts
   Council, they make a point of not being restrictive; for example
   the *Spoon River Poetry Review* urges submissions by proclaiming,
   "The editors read submissions of fine poetry from all over the
   nation and world." By and large, neither anthologies nor reviews
   take their purviews as corresponding to state boundaries.[33]
2. Bookstores and libraries. Because bookstores set up their displays to attract attention, for a subject to have its own shelf space
   means that the topic is either traditional or currently in high

---

33. The *Spoon River Poetry Review* comes out of the English Department at Illinois
State University at Normal. The quote is from their website, accessed November 24,
2005: http://www.litline.org/Spoon/about.html.

demand. Chicago bookstores usually have sections on Chicago books, often an eclectic mixture of Chicago thrillers, Nelson Algren, sociological studies, and restaurant guides. Occasionally there is a section for the Midwest. Outside of Springfield, the state capital, one never finds an "Illinois" section. Public li-. braries sometimes have an Illinois history section, but never one on Illinois writers.

    3. College and university courses. Catalogs at state universities, including the flagship campus of the University of Illinois at Urbana-Champaign, revealed not a single course on Illinois literature.

In sum, despite the fact that it is the state of Illinois—not Chicago or the multi-state Midwest—that funds and promotes a collective literary identity, one finds few traces of "Illinois literature" or "Illinois writers" as meaningful categories. The concept of an Illinois voice telling the Illinois experience is not shared by the reading public or the gatekeepers who serve it. Resources have not succeeded in creating a collective identity.

Now what about Maine? Again we focus on the state's Humanities Council as one of the principle channels for the input of State resources. The MHC's financial operations and structure are much like Illinois, only on a smaller scale, e.g., Maine has seven paid staff members compared with Illinois' eleven. About four-fifths of its cash revenues comes from the federal government in the form of NEH grants or federal matching funds, while the rest comes from private contributions, and 75–80 percent of its expenditures go to programs—grants awarded—while the rest supports administration and program development. The MHC spends roughly half as much as the IHC on grants; in 1992, Maine funded seventy-four projects with grants totaling $207,901, while that year the IHC's total was $443,684.[34]

The MHC will fund Mainers or outsiders, the key criterion being that the project is of interest to Maine people. Mainers are interested in some of the same things that interest people

---

34. These figures and the examples that follow come from the Maine Humanities Council Annual Reports, 1992 and 1993. Annual reports available from Maine Humanities Council (http://mainehumanities.org/index.php).

anywhere. So although a "Music in Baroque Culture" project gave attention to Supply Belcher, the eighteenth-century composer known as the "Handel of Maine," most of the project's music, not surprisingly, came from outside the state.[35]

If the funding pattern is any indication, however, what is of most interest to Maine people is Maine. In 1993, the MHC sponsored fourteen conferences, the largest grant going to "At Home in Wells and Ogunquit: The Home Front during World War II," which involved a public forum, collection of oral histories, and exhibition. Seven of the fourteen conferences were directly about Maine—e.g., "Northern New England Men and Women in the Civil War Era," "Maine in the Eighteenth Century," and so forth—and several others had a Maine angle, such as the one exploring Supply Belcher in the Baroque. Eight of nine exhibitions centered on Maine, the largest being "Salt and the Documentary Photography Tradition in Twentieth-Century Maine." The film/video category, in which the projects tend to be expensive, sponsored five events, all of which were about Maine. Small grants for program planning usually involved very local projects, like the $500 grant to the Island Institute for an oral-history video on the history of Cranberry Island. Overall, of the seventy-one projects supported by the MHC that year, forty-four (62 percent) were directly about Maine.

While most MHC activities support state and local consciousness, a few projects involve literary regionalism directly. One of the conferences in 1993 was Westbook College's "Giving Voice to Place: Ruth Moore's Maine" (Moore wrote novels about Maine coastal communities). The University of Maine at Presque Isle got help with their conference on "Northern Maine Writers," and the Round Top Center for the Arts in Damariscotta got $10,000 for a film on Edna St. Vincent Millay. Two years later the MHC supported the reprinting of Gladys Hasty Carroll's *As the Earth*

---

35. Belcher's musical collection *The Harmony of Maine,* published in 1794 (or twenty-six years before Maine became a state), included pieces named after Maine towns—Hallowell, York, Farmington—thus demonstrating Maine's early and persistent cultural localism.

Turns—a 1933 novel about early twentieth-century changes in Maine rural life—as part of a two-year program, in response to an NEH initiative called "The Century Project: Modern Times in Maine and America." This offers an unusually clear example of how an all-but-forgotten regionalist writer was given a boost from the cultural centers of Washington and Portland.

The MHC is clearly energetic, spending half the amount Illinois does, despite the fact that Maine has only one-tenth Illinois' population. However there hasn't been any concentrated "Read Maine" program as there has been in Illinois. Again we ask, does it work? Do people read and write Maine? Is there evidence of the growth and development of a literary collective identity nurtured by the MHC channel for State patronage? And again we look at the three indicators:

1. Anthologies and journals. Numerous anthologies of Maine writers are in print, with one or two new ones every year. The 1995–96 *Maine Writers and Publishers Alliance Catalog* listed fourteen anthologies, including large, beautifully produced collections like *Maine Speaks* and *The Maine Reader.* The state also produced an impressive number of literary journals, which both offer Maine writers a chance to be read and help consolidate the state's literary community.[36]

2. Bookstores and libraries. Of the dozens of libraries and bookstores examined, every one without exception had a section for books associated with Maine, usually located at the front of the store. Bookstores typically mix fiction and nonfiction, with books on local and state history, photographic essays, literary anthologies, and recipe books for Maine seafood all on the same shelf. Libraries usually make fiction/nonfiction distinctions on their Maine shelves, and sometimes add an additional one, with a collection on Maine and another on New England, offering regionalism at two levels. The pervasive pattern of libraries and bookstores having special Maine sections occurs not just in the tourist areas of the coast, but throughout the state.

36. These include *Beloit Poetry Journal, Café Review, Coyote's Journal, Mostly Maine, Potato Eyes, Puckerbrush Review, River Review,* and *Salt.*

3. College and university courses. The seven campuses of the University of Maine system all offer courses on Maine writers. These courses are not mandated by the state legislature or by the university system's central administration, but are the products of individual faculty initiatives.

In sum, all indicators suggest that Maine literary regionalism is flourishing. It is not clear how much state regionalism is directly due to State support. Some anthologies wouldn't exist without MHC support, and in its various activities the MHC's celebration of local writers must develop a market. Moreover, courses on Maine writers at state universities is another form of centralized (both State and state) support. What we can say with confidence is that while State support was *not* enough to develop a regional literature in Illinois, in Maine, such support appears to be promoting a regionalism that was there all along.

So as we did with Norway, we must again ask, why is literary regionalism of the reading class of Maine so much stronger than that of Illinois, especially in light of a common degree of State support and institutional encouragement? In Illinois, State funding plus strenuous efforts by the state have not developed a demand for Illinois literature, while Maine literature is a conventional and popular genre. It appears that State funding in Maine helped by conforming to a widely accepted understanding of Maine as a reasonable cultural boundary, a classification based on a shared collective identity, but the funding did not have to create the collective identity in the first place. Illinois had no such strong collective identity, and resources could not bring one into being. Why this difference in pre-existing state-level identities that could (or, in the case of Illinois, could not), under favorable conditions, be expressed in literature?

As in the Norwegian cases, much of the difference has to do the with two states' different relationships to national development. Since the mid-nineteenth century, Illinois has been emblematic of American progress: growing, attracting immigration, urbanizing. Chicago was the quintessential modern city. Illinois, part of the Midwestern "heartland," was central—culturally economically, politically, geographically—not peripheral. There was little impetus for a regional culture, for Illinois culture was American culture. Moreover, what distinctiveness there was (Chicago, the heartland) did not conform to state boundaries. Funding and promotion at the state level could not latch onto or create a cultural sense of what it meant to be "Illinois." Maine, on the other hand, was left behind in American nation building. It grew old; it lost population and saw its farms and industries wither by the late nineteenth century. Maine was and remained economically and politically different from the rest of America and even from its New England neighbors, and the state's peripheral status became deeply embedded in its collective identity. The sense of being different from other Americans operated at the state level and conformed to state boundaries. Therefore when new resources came into the literary system, they were able to engage and promote a literary culture based on Maine's cultural regionalism, something that did not exist in Illinois.

State Support and the Reading Class

It is clear that an influx of State support encourages regional literary production and awareness. However, this boost does not always produce regionalism as a collective identity that informs the choices of the reading class. State support increases the sheer volume of literary activity in a region, encourages the formation of regional organizations, and sets up communications networks that can develop the relational dimension of collective identity. All of these make a difference when the reading class has felt some prior regional identity, but they do not create one. Increased literary resources do not in and of themselves produce a regional voice. In Melucci's terms, the cognitive and emotional dimensions of the regional collective identity are independent of the relational dimension.

What establishes a robust regional collective identity, a seed that resources will allow to germinate, in the first place? The

Norwegian and American cases examined in this chapter suggest several circumstances that encourage regional cultural identity.

First, regional identity is likely to be stronger for places that are not at the center of the nation-building project. This was true for both Norwegian regions and for Maine. A region identified with the nation as a whole does not develop a strong local identity because regionalism thrives on distinction from the cultural center. An oppositional, regionalist stance becomes problematic, however, when the region takes a culturally aggressive position toward the nation as a whole. The West Coast elites in Norway saw their cultural patterns not simply as distinct from those of the Oslo area but as *more* Norwegian; Nynorsk was the extreme example of the general tendency. In such cases, the stress on local distinctiveness does not produce cultural regionalism because the region is claiming cultural centrality.

Second, regional collective identity is likely to be strong, and thus an infusion of resources is likely to make a difference, in places having small and scattered populations. Scale is important, for it takes some critical mass of a reading class to have a reading culture. Reading is correlated with education, and educated people are typically concentrated in urban centers; peripheral areas are likely to have low absolute numbers of the reading class, and the problem is exacerbated if they are scattered. In such an area, an input at the relational level can make a big difference. The Northern Norwegian Authors' Union or Maine Humanities Council mattered in a way that comparable institutions in the West Coast or Illinois did not, for they produced a critical mass of relationships and venues through which a pre-existing regional identity could be articulated.

Third, collective identities are always multiple and overlapping, so the fewer contradictions between one regional identity and some other, the better. Contradictions are debilitating. In Illinois, the gap between Chicago and downstate contradicted the "Read Illinois" concept. Moreover, there was little to distinguish downstate from neighboring Midwestern states. Illinois was doubly disadvantaged: not only was the need for relational assistance not as high as in rural Maine, but even for down-state there was not a strong cognitive or emotional dimension configured so as to take advantage of the state-level resources. Similarly, inputs directed to the Norwegian West Coast contra-dicted claims of being the "real Norway," and they did not mesh with the bourgeois Bergen's traditional mix of provinciality and cosmopolitanism. The point is not that one identity was more authentic than another, but that the configuration of new State resources did not fit the pre-existing identities.

State resources help bring regional identity—a sense of place—into articulation and exhibition, but they do not create it. Institu-tional inputs make available a representation of place, suggesting a regional frame, and the reading class—readers, writers, editors, critics, librarians, bookstore owners, educators—will accept this frame if it corresponds to a collective identity that makes sense to them. They will not accept it if it does not resonate with their experience or if it clashes with an identity they hold dear. The collective imagining of place is the result of a history of interac-tions between that place and other places, a history that may or may not produce a regional collective identity on the cognitive and emotional levels. Without this collective identity produced in and by the periphery, State inputs will prove ineffective at producing cultural regionalism. The center cannot imagine the periphery, culturally speaking, and make it stick. It can, however, enable a region that already possesses a firm collective identity to imagine itself more effectively.

Conclusion: The Reading Class and the Future of Regionalism

Reading is social. It always has been. Images of the individual lost-in-a-book reader notwithstanding, an immense apparatus—media industries; schools; religions "of the book"; vetting systems for reviewing and publicizing; bookstores and libraries and online retailers; literary prizes and festivals; reading groups; television opinion leaders; book-of-the-month clubs; social honors; "One city, One book" programs—supports the favorite pastime of the reading class.[1]

Reading is an elite practice. It almost always has been. The era of middle- and working-class readers that lasted in the West from the mid-nineteenth to mid-twentieth century was historically exceptional. Members of the reading class are socially powerful, with influence disproportionate to their numbers. The reading class exerts its influence through its social, cultural, and political

1. Regarding numerous early-modern depictions of fathers reading the Bible to their children, the historian Robert Darnton remarks that "[F]or all their sentimentality, such descriptions proceed from a common assumption: for the common people in early modern Europe, reading was a social activity. It took place in workshops, barns, and taverns. It was almost always oral but not necessarily edifying" Darnton (1990, 168).

participation. "Literary readers are more likely than non-literary readers to perform volunteer and charity work, visit art museums, attend performing arts events, and attend sporting events." Readers are cultural omnivores, doing more of almost all forms of cultural activity except watching television. Readers vote more. Readers are active in their communities. Readers possess and exercise social capital.[2]

Why does the practice of reading, over and above education, have these effects? Four independent features of reading play a role. The first is that reading, unlike many other pastimes, serves as a source of information (knowledge is power), while at the same time it offers a ready-to-hand medium for disseminating information, opinions, ideas, and calls to action (recall Shirley, the Lancaster community activist in Barton and Hamilton's study, who uses literacy "to get things done"). Second, reading gives rise to formal and informal discussion groups, such as book clubs. "Intense personal, intellectual, and occasionally even political bonds are forged in these lively discussions. Regular participants become more involved in wider community affairs . . . In short, by converting a solitary intellectual activity (reading) into one that is social and even civic, discussion groups provide a fertile forcing bed for both *schmoozers* and *machers*." Third, reading carries social honor, which is why everyone from presidential candidates to Hollywood celebrities gets asked about their reading. Fourth, reading can carve out a private space and time, and this can be renewing and even empowering (recall Radway's romance fans insisting that their husbands watch the kids during their reading time).[3]

A historical study of Jewish women in Eastern Europe illustrates the empowering effect of reading. According to Iris Parush, nineteenth-century Jewish communities witnessed intense ideological debate between traditional rabbis (*haredim*) and

2. "Literary readers . . ." quotation is from National Endowment for the Arts (2004a, xii). For the social capital of reading groups, see Putnam (2000, 149–50).

3. "Intense personal . . ." quotation is from Putnam (2000, 149).

modernizing intellectuals (*maskelim*). These communities were trilingual (Hebrew, Yiddish, and the state language). But the languages were unevenly distributed: women were largely excluded from Hebrew, while the *maskelim* avoided writing in European languages because they did not want outsiders to see any internal conflicts. So the readership for modern, secular, European-language Jewish literature consisted of women, who were marginalized from the intellectual debate. Gender roles encouraged couples to marry young, with women as the breadwinners while men studied the Torah; this arrangement both gave women freedom and required competence in European languages. Education contributed to the gender differences: boys learned to read in schools, where all the emphasis was on mastering Hebrew, while girls (not expected to accomplish much intellectually) learned to read privately and in European languages. They were "marginal" to the Jewish educational project, and their education was of lower prestige, but this marginality left them free to pursue different forms of reading and learning. As Parush sums it up:

> Without understating in the slightest the difficulties and hindrances that were the lot of many women, one cannot at the same time ignore the degree of freedom and the empowering resources that this realm of marginality granted many of them. The status of many women as breadwinners, along with the matrimonial practices, the attitude of traditional society toward the education of women, and the content and practices in the cultural sphere women occupied—all these supplied women with great advantages for the encounter with modernity. This space, contemptuously regarded and for the most part left unsupervised by traditional society, opened unexpected possibilities for many of the women—to utilize their skills in literacy and to influence their surroundings. More than a few women began to set in motion processes that were, from the perspective of traditional society, unexpected and undesirable.

Parush notes that although *Maskelim* might have been expected to approve of these modern women, they were ambivalent or even hostile, sensing a threat to hierarchy represented by these new entrants into the reading class.[4]

The fact that virtually every notable accomplishment from winning the Tour de France to serving as Secretary of State gives rise to a book describing how it was done and what it was like attests to the prestige of reading and people's desire to impress the reading class. And while the phenomenon of celebrity books and political memoirs is often remarked upon, what is less often noticed is how the accomplishment-to-book movement goes only in one direction. Bill Gates or Madonna or Margaret Thatcher or Ted Kennedy feel compelled to produce books, but authors rarely feel compelled to design software or sing or run for office. It seems as if, regardless of their wealth or power, celebrated individuals enhance their cultural prestige—at least in the eyes of the reading class—by writing (or having someone else write) a book.

The interplay between books and celebrities goes beyond autobiographies and memoirs. Stars are drawn into the world of books. Moviegoers may think the actor Hugh Grant's closest contact with literature was when he played an independent bookstore owner in *Notting Hill*, but he is said to be "an Oxford-educated English scholar" who was named a judge for the 2004 Whitbread Book of the Year. An article reporting this mentions the movies that Grant has starred in, including *Bridget Jones's Diary*. Bridget had a print history long before her film adventures, first as a humorous column written by Helen Fielding for *The Independent*, then as a novel (1996), then as the film (2001), and then in 2004 a celebrated actor from the film was chosen to judge books. And the circle continues: books that win Whitbread and other prizes get publicity and increase their odds of being made into films. Such interweaving of books with other media is just one of the consequences of reading being both socially embedded and prestigious.[5]

4. Parush (2004); the quotation is from p. 70.
5. Van Gelder (2004).

The Reading Class and Reading Culture[6]

Within a literate society, there is a core of people who read a lot. These are the people who always have a book with them, who use libraries, who have books in every room of their homes, who buy books, who read book reviews, who have magazines and paperbacks littering their cars, who keep a bookmark for Amazon.com on their Internet browsers. They tend to be self-conscious of themselves as "readers," and are somewhat contemptuous of non-readers, by whom they mean not illiterates, but people who share their educational and economic qualifications but seldom read in their leisure time.

These people constitute the reading class. A reading class is not the same as a reading culture. The distinction between the two is important for regional literature, because regional literature requires a reading class, but it does not necessarily require a reading culture. A reading culture is a place (a city, a province, a country) where most people, over and above the demands of their job or schooling, routinely read printed materials for entertainment and information. Reading cultures are rare and becoming rarer.

Reading cultures always have reading classes, but reading classes often flourish without reading cultures. Reading classes are old, for there have long been coteries of scribes and priests and aristocrats who read and use written communication. Reading cultures are recent, arising in the commercial towns long before most people in the hinterlands were literate. It is common to have a reading class without having a reading culture. China during the Qing dynasty was administered by a reading class, the bureaucratic literati, but most Chinese neither had the capacity to read nor the desire to. The scribal-manuscript culture of medieval Europe, or the Koran-based cultures of conservative Islamic societies past and present, offer clear examples of elite reading classes without reading cultures.

6. Some of this section is drawn from Griswold (2001).

Where reading starts to penetrate public life rather than remaining within bureaucratic, clerical, or scholarly ghettos, a reading culture may emerge. Historically this has happened first in commercial centers. Signs of a reading culture include the invention of written "news" produced for and consumed by an anonymous "public"; signage, graffiti, and other impersonal messages on city streets; and the appearance of written forms of popular entertainment. We see the early stages of a reading culture in imperial Rome, in West African market towns during the end of the colonial period, in Shanghai during the first two decades of the twentieth century, and in late sixteenth-century London.[7]

If a people are developing, or seem likely to develop, a reading culture, pressures for mass education emerge, for literacy starts becoming a requirement for full social participation. In an established reading culture, there is a rough but direct association between the prestige of a job and the amount of reading it requires. Moreover, reading for entertainment takes place at most social levels, with reading materials stratified from *belles lettres* for the highbrows to comics, pamphlets, and *fotonovelas* for the semi-literate. In a reading culture, what one reads is a way by which people gauge social status.

Just as the presence of a reading class does not guarantee a reading culture, a reading class may remain robust while its surrounding reading culture atrophies. Something of this sort happened in Nigeria during the last quarter of the twentieth century, where economic collapse destroyed the market for books and

---

7. Reading cultures do not invariably take hold, however. In Rome, reading remained strictly an urban activity, and no more than 20–30% of Roman men and 10% of Roman women ever achieved literacy. This type of restricted urban literacy been called a craftsmen's literacy, broader in base than the scribal literacy of the clerics and bureaucrats, but far from popular. In West Africa the faltering economies and political upheavals of the last half of the twentieth century have produced a decline in education and in the reading habit. Even in England the rate of literacy may have been lower in 1700 than it was in 1600. But in nineteenth-century London or early twentieth-century Shanghai, the commercialization of reading materials offset threats to the nascent reading culture, and something more like a mass reading public was established. See Harris (1989) and Link (1981).

damaged the educational infrastructure that had been producing new demand. Members of the class fraction that constituted the reading class—affluent, largely southern, Christian, and educated, people who had been the backbone of the indigenous administration under colonialism—continued to buy their books in London and New York, while the popular readership declined. Moreover, reading was no longer key to economic success; in an oil-based economy where personal access to the regime was the route to wealth and power, reading skills and habits became largely irrelevant. The reading class remains, but it is isolated. "We do not yet have a reading culture," discouraged writers and booksellers admit, adding hopefully, "but someday we will." In Europe and the United States something similar may be taking place: the reading class is robust, but increasingly concentrated in a highly educated slice of the society, while the reading culture is stagnant.[8]

What are the implications of this distinction between a reading class and a reading culture? Two predictions seem justified: First, books will retain immense prestige because of the status of the reading class. An apparatus of publicity sees to it that books are "known" well beyond those who have actually read them; an apparatus of educational institutions sees to it that the practice of reading is honored. These are not about to change. Books will in all likelihood continue to be the single most effective means of influencing the public agenda by reaching members of the educated elite via the reading class. And the reading class, always inclined to look down upon those who could read but don't, may even increase its prestige as reading loses its hold on the majority of people. The concentration effect discussed in chapter 2, whereby fewer people read but readers are more avid and more self-aware, will ensure this.

Second, social categories that have not been part of the reading class to date are unlikely to join it in the future, nor will a reading culture emerge in places that do not already have one. This will

8. See Griswold (2000) for the social history of Nigerian reading culture.

not be because people cannot read or do not read on the job, but because they do not feel the desire to read in their leisure time. The Nigerian reading class that looks forward to a broad reading culture in the future will probably be disappointed. In Europe and North America the reading class is educated, affluent, white, middle aged, and tilted toward women. Most members of minority groups, most less educated people, many younger people and especially young men are unlikely to pick up the book habit. They get their information, entertain themselves, and mold their opinions through traditional (word-of-mouth; community leaders; popular music) and newer (broadcast media; Internet; blogs; podcasting) sources. And in those countries that have not yet developed a reading culture, the reading class will continue to be prestigious, but somewhat isolated from the mainstream.

Numerical predictions are hazardous, but I will venture a couple. In the West and Japan, the reading class will stabilize at something between one-quarter and one-third of the population. It will vary—Norway's will remain larger than Italy's—but overall that will be the picture: a minority, but a good-sized minority, of adults will read in their spare time. In developing countries the reading class will be a smaller minority, perhaps around 15 percent. The reading class will remain strong, but the day of the reading culture is over.

Reading-Class Desire and the Future of Regionalism

One of the ways in which the reading class exerts its cultural influence is by perpetuating regionalism. Members of the reading class become regionalists and supporters for regional literature not because they have to, but because they chose to. Unearthing the cultural roots of a place is a way members of the reading class put down their own roots. Cowbirds move into the local cultural nest and make themselves at home. Reading-class cosmopolitans "do localism" as a way of confirming and deepening one of the identity dimensions which they have selected for themselves.

To describe the process this way is to suggest that it is artificial, which it is, and phony, which it isn't. All culture is artificial by definition, for it is the result of human thought and practice, not of some inexorable natural process. And the quest for cultural authenticity is a snipe hunt. What has been constructed and institutionalized a few generations back appears authentic, but historians and anthropologists routinely deconstruct seemingly primordial cultural patterns. Authenticity confers value, but people confer authenticity on what they value in the first place. There is nothing extraordinary about this. The so-called invention of tradition is simply a speed-up, giving attention to the normal process of cultural creation and transmission. This is particularly the case for literature, which depends on print media, and therefore on an industrial apparatus and a complex society. So when a member of the reading class goes local—learning about, supporting, promoting all things regional, regardless of the fact that she may have come from someplace else—this cowbird is no more or less of a cultural phony than anyone else who embraces some form of cultural expression.

Regional literature results from a reading class having cognitive, emotional, and relational interests as well as material and educational resources. The conditions have to be favorable for the reading class to promote regionalism. The cases examined in the previous chapters demonstrate that the impulse toward regional identification is less likely to result in regional literature when the reading class's identification with a particular region is weak in the first place (Illinois), or when the cultural identification with the region conflicts with another valued identification (West Norway), or when the reading class is committed to a universal ideology (Italy), or when the identification with the region is politically awkward (liberals in the American South), or when the market for regional writing is small and there is no state or other form of patronage to subsidize the regionalist voice (Italy). On the other hand, where there are guarantees of state or private support, where the regional sense of cultural distinction is longstanding, and where there are few political or market costs to be paid, the reading class helps regionalism endure.

This regionalism is as much a new creation as it is a leftover. Recall (in chapter 3) Raymond Williams's classification of culture as dominant, alternative, residual, or emergent. Regionalism "endures" as residual culture, of course, but it also reemerges, as for example when educators rediscover and teach long-forgotten local authors. More striking still, regionalism can be a new creation. The New England town green offers a non-literary example. Historian Stephen Nissenbaum writes that the "pastoralization" of town commons—previously these had been bare patches, rather like parking lots—didn't take place until after Civil War, when local Village Improvement Societies, dominated by businessmen who often were newcomers to the community, began to plant grass and elm trees. Litchfield, Connecticut, actually hired Frederick Law Olmstead, designer of Central Park, to "restore" their common. Likewise in literature, it is often newcomers—cowbirds—who rediscover and even create regionalism, consuming and in some cases producing "the local." A typical example is when the authors included in an anthology of contemporary Maine women writers gathered together, they discovered that none had actually been born in Maine. Thus does the reading class support literary regionalism, reading it and sometimes writing it as well.[9]

Paradoxical as it seems, the complex systems and technological capacities of the contemporary period make it easier for the reading class to enact its local-culture aspirations. For example, say a cowbird has moved to Winnipeg and now wants to settle into the local culture by, among other things, becoming familiar with books set in Manitoba and with local authors. Perhaps she will browse the displays in the local library or bookstores, where such books will be featured prominently. The cowbird

9. Nissenbaum (1996). The anthology was *The Eloquent Edge: 15 Maine Women Writers* (Bar Harbor: Acadia Press, 1995); I am grateful to Patricia O'Donnell, author and English professor at the University of Maine at Farmington, for this account.

may already have some titles in mind, having read a review in the *Winnipeg Free Press,* heard an author on local radio, or talked with her new neighbors about joining a book group.

Now let's say that our cowbird lives some distance from a library or bookstore. Like everyone else, she turns to the Internet for the information she wants, and, as studies by Eszter Hargittai and others have amply documented, highly educated people like the members of the reading class are skilled at finding what they want online with minimal effort.[10] She might go to the City of Winnipeg home page, the first thing that pops up if she Googles Winnipeg (she's probably consulted it already for other area information). A couple of clicks gets her to the literary page, under "Film and Cultural Affairs," where she learns about:

- "The Association of Manitoba Book Publishers (AMBP), [which represents] a diverse group of Manitoba publishing houses [and] coordinates joint marketing projects such as Prairie Books NOW (a magazine dedicated to Prairie publishers and writers) and Manitoba Book Week (a week-long celebration of Manitoba publishing); and advocates for the continued evolution of one of Manitoba's most culturally dynamic industries—publishing.
- "The Manitoba Book Awards are presented annually at Brave New Words, the Manitoba Writing and Publishing Awards gala held in spring which caps off Manitoba Book Week. The 15 awards are presented for works in French and English, including the City of Winnipeg's $5,000 prize, the Carol Shields Winnipeg Book Award.
- "In 1999 the City of Winnipeg established its first book award. The first Carol Shields Winnipeg Book Award was presented in 2000 at Brave New Words, the Manitoba Literary Awards. The Award is a juried annual prize honouring books which evoke the special character, and contribute to the appreciation and understanding of Winnipeg.
- "For readers, the Winnipeg International Writers Festival is the place to experience the written word firsthand and meet writers from home and abroad. The Festival features writers from all genres presented in a variety of venues."

10. Hargittai (2002).

Perhaps she will simple Google "Manitoba" and "fiction." Up comes Great Plains Publications, which announces itself to be an "independent, Winnipeg-based book publisher specializing in Prairie history, biography, and fiction." Here she can consider recent titles in suspense, literary fiction, and juvenile fiction, most by authors from Manitoba, and most set there.

Or she might go to Amazon.com for recommendations. A search of "Manitoba" and "fiction" comes up with eleven titles, like *Made in Manitoba: An Anthology of Short Fiction* (Kroetsch, Birdsell, and Roy) and a western called *Manitoba Marauders* (Sharpe). "Winnipeg fiction" comes up with eleven suggestions, "Manitoba poetry" and "Manitoba authors" with five each, and so forth. Or she might take a look at the Amazon.com Purchase Circle for Manitoba to see what the locals are reading. Amazon.com has no end of advice for her.

Where do all of these Manitoba books come from? Local writers' organizations and publishing help produce a steady stream of regionalism, and much of these are sponsored by the State, at the provincial or central level. Great Plains Publications is happy to announce its many public benefactors: "Great Plains acknowledges the support of the Canada Council for the Arts, Canadian Heritage, the Manitoba Arts Council and the Manitoba Department of Culture, Heritage and Tourism." A novice writer might go to the city website and learn about:

- The Manitoba Writers' Guild, "a grassroots organization created by and for Manitoba writers. Our goal is to discover, develop and promote literary talent province wide."
- "Prairie Fire magazine publishes new work by both emerging and established writers. Each issue is loaded with stories, poems and articles to engage the mind and enrich your spirit."
- The Writer's Collective, which offers "programs and services for professional and developing writers . . . [and] provides writer's circles, workshops, lecture series and a bi-monthly journal."

And so forth. Writers find many opportunities of this sort through which they can network with other Manitoba writers and develop a sense of collective identity at the regional level.[11]

Writers that live in or write about Manitoba may or may not define themselves as "Manitoba (or Winnipeg) writers," regardless of their participation in local networks. They may or may not constitute a cultural movement, a shared collective identity, as discussed in chapter 5. They may or may not follow the regionalist aesthetic. Regardless of whether they embrace this regionalist definition, however, literary institutions—bookstores and libraries, Amazon.com, the Winnipeg International Literary Festival, reading group's and anthologies—will frame them as such.

One of the most powerful institutional framers is the Library of Congress's practice of assigning subject headings. Up until the 1990s, the Library of Congress (LOC) gave subject headings only to nonfiction titles and to a few select categories, like biographical fiction. Catalogers increasingly felt the need to begin using such headings for fiction, and after a decade of considerable experimentation, the Library of Congress's subject headings for fiction became permanent policy in 1999. The traditional LOC attitude remains, however, that not too much time should be spent on literature subject headings, for these are really for nonfiction. Because of this, although ten is the maximum number of subject headings that the Library allows, for literature the cataloger usually uses far fewer, usually three or four, such as the four used for Annie Proulx's novel, *That Old Ace in the Hole*, shown in figure 10.[12]

Setting is one of the headings used most often. This is the case because (1) the catalogers think it is an important feature of the novel, and (2) it is something that can be ascertained very

11. The Manitoba URLs are: http://www.winnipeg.ca/interhom/; http://www.winnipeg.ca/filmandculture/literary/default.stm; http://www.greatplains.mb.ca/index.php. Such websites, which change all the time, typify the online resources available to a cowbird in Manitoba.

12. I am immensely grateful to Susan Haddock, Librarian (Cataloging), Senior Cataloguer at the Library of Congress, who allowed me to observe how the subject-heading system worked.

That old ace in the hole : a novel / Annie Proulx.
LC Control No.:   2002030462
Type of Material: Book (Print, Microform, Electronic, etc.)
Personal Name: Proulx, Annie.
Main Title: That old ace in the hole : a novel / Annie Proulx.
Published/Created: New York : Scribner, c2002.
Description: xii, 361 p. ; 25 cm.
ISBN: 0684813076 (alk. paper)
Subjects: Young men--Fiction.
        Oklahoma Panhandle (Okla.)--Fiction.
        Texas Panhandle (Tex.)--Fiction.
        Denver (Colo.)--Fiction.
Form/Genre: Bildungsromans. gsafd
LC Classification: PS3566.R697 T48 2002
Dewey Class No.:   813/.54 21
Geographic Area Code: n-us-co n-us-tx n-us-ok

FIGURE 10. Subject headings for *That Old Ace in the Hole*

quickly. The cataloger with the primary responsibility for fiction subject headings does not actually read the novels. She skims them, along with the materials sent by the publisher, and comes up with the subject headings for thirty to fifty books each and every day. Given this workflow, place is something easy to spot and assign.

The assignment has implications extending far beyond the Library of Congress. As is true for *The Old Ace in the Hole,* the subject headings appear on the back of the title page of most books, exactly as the LOC has conceived of them. Most libraries use the LOC headings. So do retailers. As figure 10 shows, *That Old Ace in the Hole* has "Oklahoma Panhandle—Fiction" as one of its subject headings. If one searches Amazon.com for "Oklahoma Panhandle fiction," up pops the title. Google produces the same. Thus does the quick decisions made by a single cataloguer in Washington permeate the literary world and perpetuate Panhandle regionalism.

Regionalism resonates with the wished-for identities of the reading class. It offers the pleasure of roots to the rootless. Members of the reading class are rich with options, and they have the resources, the cultural and material capital, through which they can enact their choices. They are masters of the complex institutional systems and informational technologies that enable them to put together their chosen cultural worlds. These worlds often are constructed on a foundation of place. In literature, they run toward rural settings, wise-but-unsophisticated characters, suspicion of outsiders, pastoral escapism, nature and weather and geology and all of the other features that make up the regionalist aesthetic. This aesthetic resonates not with the reading class's experience, but with its desires.

That being the case, the future of regionalism looks bright. Not only do information technologies and institutional systems enable the identification and promotion of regional literature, but privileged people want it. The reading class tends to get what it wants.

As I was writing this, I glanced at the day's *New York Times* Travel section, which comes out every Friday and which contains a regular feature called "36 Hours" that tells *Times* readers how to spend a perfect weekend someplace. That January 27, 2006, perfect day-and-a-half was in Whitehorse, in the Yukon Territory. The article begins: "In *The Spell of the Yukon*, the Klondike bard Robert W. Service wrote of the beauty and serenity of the 'great big, broad land 'way up yonder.' Spend a winter weekend in Whitehorse, and you'll find that the spell is truly contagious." The article goes on to recommend hour-by-hour activities that include dogsled excursions, spots for viewing the northern lights, an Italian restaurant, and a coffee house that features "the works of local artists and a seven-ounce bag of chocolate-covered coffee beans ($4.50), which dog mushers eat on the trail to say alert." At 3 p.m. on Saturday, it suggests that the reader go "prospecting for books" at Mac's Fireweed Books, "a Yukon-centric bookstore with an extensive stock of classic and contemporary works by the North's men and women of letters," which it then proceeds to name: Robert W. Service, Jack London, Pierre Berton.[13]

13. Mackin (2006).

Travel, restaurants, art, coffee shops, bookstores, and regional writers: the combination is so ubiquitous as to be unremarkable, even unseen. Members of the reading class—and most *New York Times* readers would be book-carrying members—fashion their leisure time around such pursuits and pleasures. So do most readers of this book. Such cosmopolitans and cowbirds ensure that regionalism and the regionalist aesthetic will endure, just as regionalism offers the reading class a cultural mooring to anchor and orient them in a tumultuous world.

Appendix A: Authors from Survey2000

A. General Authors: Thirty Well-Known American Writers Not Associated with a Specific State

Some of these writers are associated with a large region—e.g., Louis L'Amour with the West. Some do in fact write about a certain territory—e.g., John Grisham sets most of his legal thrillers in Memphis or Mississippi, and Stephen King sets many of his in Maine. They are on this list either because they are not strongly associated with any one state, or because their fame or popularity is such that we expected that their state association was probably irrelevant.

1. James Baldwin
2. Russell Banks
3. Mary Higgins Clark
4. Stephen Crane
5. Pat Conroy
6. Robertson Davies
7. Emily Dickinson
8. Joy Fielding
9. F. Scott Fitzgerald

10. Allen Ginsberg
11. John Grisham
12. Robert Heinlein
13. John Irving
14. Jan Karon
15. Jack Kerouac
16. Stephen King
17. Dean Koontz
18. Louis L'Amour
19. Herman Melville
20. Frank Norris
21. Joyce Carol Oates
22. Marge Peircy
23. Annie Proulx
24. Anna Quindlan
25. Nora Roberts
26. Anne Rivers Siddons
27. Danielle Steel
28. Alice Walker
29. Edith Wharton
30. Richard Wright

B. Authors Associated with Specific States, Clustered by Census Regions

NEW ENGLAND

Connecticut: Rose Terry Cooke; Wallace Stevens
Maine: R. P. T. Coffin; Sarah Orne Jewett; Edna St. Vincent Millay; Edwin Arlington Robinson; Tim Sample
Massachusetts: Henry Adams; Anne Bradstreet; Nathaniel Hawthorne; Robert B. Parker; Henry David Thoreau
New Hampshire: Alice Brown; Robert Frost; Celia Thaxter
Rhode Island: Avi; A. J. Liebling; H. P. Lovecraft; Roger Williams
Vermont: Robert Newton Peck; Rowland Evans Robinson

MID-ATLANTIC

New Jersey: Joyce Kilmer; William Carlos Williams
New York: . H. C. Bunner; Philander Deming; Harold Frederic;

O. Henry; Washington Irving; Tama Janowitz; Brander Matthews; Jay McInerney; Richard Russo

Pennsylvania: Charles Brockden Brown; K. C. Constantine; John Edgar Wideman

EAST NORTH CENTRAL

Illinois: Gwendolyn Brooks; John Hay; Joseph Kirkland; David Mamet; Edgar Lee Masters; William Maxwell; Sara Paretsky; Carl Sandberg

Indiana: Edward Eggleston; James Whitcomb Riley; Booth Tarkington

Michigan: Charles Baxter; Elmore Leonard

Ohio: Sherwood Anderson; Mary Hartwell Catherwood; Toni Morrison; Constance Fenimore Woolson

Wisconsin: Zona Gale; Hamlin Garland

WEST NORTH CENTRAL

Iowa: Bess Streeter Aldrich; Jane Smiley

Kansas: Ed (E. W.) Howe; Hendle Rumbaut

Minnesota: Garrison Keillor; Sinclair Lewis

Missouri: Richard E. Brown; Mark Twain

Nebraska: Willa Cather; Wright Morris

North Dakota: Era Bell Thompson; Larry Woiwode

South Dakota: Frederick Manfred; Ole Rolvagg; Laura Ingalls Wilder

SOUTH ATLANTIC

Delaware: Jennifer Ackerman; Frank Dale; David J. Seibold

Florida: Zora Neale Hurston; John D. MacDonald; Marjorie Kinnan Rawlings; Bob Shacochis

Georgia: Joes Chandler Harris; Margaret Mitchell; Carson McCullers; Flannery O'Connor

Maryland: John Barth; H. L. Mencken; Anne Tyler

North Carolina: Charles W. Chesnutt; Jill McCorkle; Thomas Wolfe

South Carolina: Dorothy Allison; Blanche McCrary Boyd

Virginia: John Pendleton Kennedy; Thomas Nelson Page

Washington, DC: Ward Just; Margaret Truman; Marcella Comes Winslow

West Virginia: Denise Giardina; Mary Lee Settle

EAST SOUTH CENTRAL
  Alabama: Mary Ward Brown; Julia Fields
  Kentucky: Wendell Berry; John Fox; Robert Penn Warren
  Mississippi: William Faulkner; Eudora Welty; Tennessee Williams
  Tennessee: Mary N. Murfree (pseud. Charles Egbert Craddock);
    John Crowe Ransom; Allen Tate

WEST SOUTH CENTRAL
  Arkansas: Henry Dumas; Joan Hess
  Oklahoma: Rilla Askew; Will Rogers
  Louisiana: George Washington Cable; Kate Chopin; Anne Rice
  Texas: Benjamin Franklin Capps; L. Frank Dobie; Molly Ives; Frank
    Kea; Cormac McCarthy; Larry McMurtry

MOUNTAIN
  Arizona: Zane Grey: Barbara Kingsolver; Alfred Henry Lewis
  Colorado: Gene Amole; Sanora Babb; Helen Hunt Jackson
  Idaho: Ernest Hemingway; James H. Maguire
  Montana: Peter Bowen; Ivan Doig; A. B. Guthrie Jr.; Norman Maclean
  Nevada: Walter Van Tilburg Clark
  New Mexico: Mary Austin; S. Omar Barker; Tony Hillerman; Leslie
    Marmon Silko
  Utah: Edward Abbey; Bernard De Voto; Zane Grey; Terry Tem-
    pleton Williams
  Wyoming: Gretel Erlich; Ron Franscell; Mary O'Hara

PACIFIC
  Alaska: Rex Beach; John Haines; Robert W. Service
  California: Raymond Chandler; Ernest J. Finney; Bret Harte; Jack
    London; Ross MacDonald; Armistead Maupin; Joaquin Miller;
    Wallace Stegner; John Steinbeck
  Hawaii: Joseph Joel Keith; James Michener; Cathy Song
  Oregon: Don Berry; Francis Parkman Jr.; Elizabeth Woody
  Washington: Earl Emerson; David Guterson

Appendix B: Most Popular Authors Overall and in Nine Regions (Top Fifteen in Each Category, Ordered According to Popularity)

Overall

Mark Twain
Ernest Hemingway
John Steinbeck
Robert Frost
Emily Dickinson
Stephen King
Henry David Thoreau
Nathaniel Hawthorne
Jack London
F. Scott Fitzgerald
John Grisham
William Faulkner
Tennessee Williams

James Michener
Laura Ingalls Wilder

New England

Mark Twain
Robert Frost
Ernest Hemingway
John Steinbeck
Henry David Thoreau
Nathaniel Hawthorne
Emily Dickinson
Stephen King
F. Scott Fitzgerald
Jack London
John Grisham
William Faulkner
Herman Melville
Tennessee Williams
Washington Irving

Middle Atlantic

Mark Twain
Ernest Hemingway
Robert Frost
John Steinbeck
Emily Dickinson
F. Scott Fitzgerald
Nathaniel Hawthorne
Stephen King
Henry David Thoreau
Jack London
William Faulkner
John Grisham
Tennessee Williams
O. Henry
Washington Irving

East North Central

Mark Twain
Ernest Hemingway
Robert Frost
John Steinbeck
Emily Dickinson
Stephen King
Nathaniel Hawthorne
Henry David Thoreau
F. Scott Fitzgerald
John Grisham
Jack London
Carl Sandburg
William Faulkner
Tennessee Williams
Laura Ingalls Wilder

West North Central

Mark Twain
Ernest Hemingway
Robert Frost
Laura Ingalls Wilder
John Steinbeck
Stephen King
Emily Dickinson
F. Scott Fitzgerald
Henry David Thoreau
Jack London
John Grisham
Nathaniel Hawthorne
Garrison Keillor
Sinclair Lewis
James Michener

South Atlantic

Mark Twain
Ernest Hemingway
Robert Frost
John Steinbeck
Emily Dickinson
Stephen King
John Grisham
F. Scott Fitzgerald
Henry David Thoreau
Nathaniel Hawthorne
Jack London
William Faulkner
Tennessee Williams
Herman Melville
Carl Sandburg

East South Central

Mark Twain
Robert Frost
Ernest Hemingway
Emily Dickinson
John Steinbeck
William Faulkner
John Grisham
Tennessee Williams
Stephen King
F. Scott Fitzgerald
Henry David Thoreau
Nathaniel Hawthorne
Jack London
Carl Sandburg
O. Henry

West South Central

Mark Twain
Ernest Hemingway
Emily Dickinson
John Steinbeck
Robert Frost
Stephen King
Nathaniel Hawthorne
William Faulkner
John Grisham
Jack London
F. Scott Fitzgerald
Tennessee Williams
Henry David Thoreau
Will Rogers
James Michener

Mountain

Mark Twain
John Steinbeck
Ernest Hemingway
Robert Frost
Jack London
Stephen King
Emily Dickinson
Henry David Thoreau
James Michener
John Grisham
F. Scott Fitzgerald
Laura Ingalls Wilder
Nathaniel Hawthorne
William Faulkner
Tennessee Williams

Pacific

Mark Twain
John Steinbeck
Ernest Hemingway
Robert Frost
Jack London
Emily Dickinson
John Grisham
Henry David Thoreau
Stephen King
James Michener
F. Scott Fitzgerald
Nathaniel Hawthorne
William Faulkner
Herman Melville
Laura Ingalls Wilder

References

Allum, Percy. 1990. "Uniformity Undone: Aspects of Catholic Culture in Postwar Italy." Ch. 4 in Barański and Lumley 1990, 79–96.

Alpers, Paul. 1996. *What is Pastoral?* Chicago: University of Chicago Press.

Altick, Richard D. 1957. *The English Common Reader: A Social History of the Mass Reading Public, 1800–1900.* Chicago: University of Chicago Press.

Amtower, Laurel. 2000. *Engaging Words: The Culture of Reading in the Later Middle Ages.* New York: Palgrave/St. Martin's Press.

Andersen, Jenny, and Elizabeth Sauer, eds. 2002. *Books and Readers in Early Modern England: Material Studies.* Philadelphia: University of Pennsylvania Press.

Anderson, Benedict. (1983) 1991. *Imagined Communities: Reflections on the Origin and Spread of Nationalism.* Rev. ed. London: Verso.

Anderson, Elijah. 1999. *Code of the Street: Decency, Violence, and the Moral Life of the Inner City.* New York: W. W. Norton.

Anghelescu, Hermina G. B., and Martine Poulain, eds. 2001. *Books, Libraries, Reading, and Publishing in the Cold War.* Washington, DC: Library of Congress, Center for the Book.

Asor Rosa, Alberto. 1989. "Centralismo e policentrismo nella letterature italiana unitaria." In *Letteratura italiana: Storia e geografia.* Vol. terzo: L'eta contemporanea, 5–74. Torino: Giulio Einaudi.

Ayers, Edward L., Patricia Nelson Limerick, Stephen Nissenbaum, and Peter S. Onuf. 1996. *All Over the Map: Rethinking American Regions.* Baltimore: Johns Hopkins University Press.

Bagnasco, Arnaldo. 1977. *Tre Italie: La Problematica Territoriale dello Sviluppo Italiano.* Bologna: Il Mulino.

Barański, Zygmunt G. 1990. "Pier Paolo Pasolini: Culture, Croce, Gramsci." Ch. 7 in Barański and Lumley 1990, 139–59.

Barański, Zygmunt G., and Robert Lumley, eds. 1990. *Culture and Conflict in Postwar Italy: Essays on Mass and Popular Culture.* Houndmills: Macmillan.

Barron, Hal S. 1984. *Those Who Stayed Behind: Rural Society in Nineteenth-Century New England.* New York: Cambridge University Press.

Barton, David, and Mary Hamilton. 1998. *Local Literacies: Reading and Writing in One Community.* London: Routledge.

Becker, Howard S. 1982. *Art Worlds.* Berkeley: University of California Press.

Bhabha, Homi K. 1994. *The Location of Culture.* London: Routledge.

Birkerts, Sven. 1994. *The Gutenberg Elegies: The Fate of Reading in an Electronic Age.* Boston: Faber and Faber.

Blumenthal, Ralph. 2005. "College Libraries Set Aside Books in a Digital Age." *New York Times.* May 14.

Bonifazi, Corrado, Luigi Costanzo, Costanza Giovannelli, and Frank Heins. 2005. "Investigating Labour Market Determinants of Italian Internal Migration Flows 1997–2001 (draft)." Presented at the International Union for the Scientific Study of Population, XXV International Population Conference, Tours, France.

Book Marketing Ltd. 2000. *Reading the Situation: Book Reading, Buying and Borrowing Habits in Britain.* London: Book Marketing/The Reading Partnership.

Bourdieu, Pierre. 1979. *La distinction: critique sociale du jugement.* Paris: Éditions de Minuit.

The Bowker Annual Library and Book Trade Almanac. 1996. New York: R. R. Bowker.

Brand, Peter, and Lino Pertile, eds. 1996. *The Cambridge History of Italian Literature.* Cambridge: Cambridge University Press.

Brandt, Deborah. 2001. *Literacy in American Lives.* Cambridge: Cambridge University Press.

Brockmeier, Jens, Min Wang, and David R. Olson. 2002. *Literacy, Narrative, and Culture*. Richmond, Surrey, U.K.: Curzon.

Brooks, Jeffrey. 1985. *When Russia Learned to Read: Literacy and Popular Literature, 1861–1917*. Princeton: Princeton University Press.

Bryson, Bethany. 1996. "'Anything But Heavy Metal': Symbolic Exclusion and Musical Dislikes." *American Sociological Review* 61:884–99.

Burke, Peter. 1978. *Popular Culture in Early Modern Europe*. New York: Harper & Row.

Butler, Richard J., Benjamin W. Cowan, and Sebastian Nilsson. 2005. "From Obscurity to Bestseller: Examining the Impact of Oprah's Book Club Selections." *Publishing Research Quarterly* 20(4): 23–34.

Buzzeo, Toni, and Jane Kurtz. 2002. *35 Best Books for Teaching U.S. Regions: Using Fiction to Help Students Explore the Geography, History, and Cultures of the Seven U.S. Regions—and Link Literature to Social Studies*. New York: Scholastic (Professional Books).

Caesar, Michael, and Hainsworth, Peter, eds. 1984. *Writers and Society in Contemporary Italy: A Collection of Essays*. Leamington Spa, Warwickshire: Berg Publishers.

Castells, Manuel. 1989. *The Informational City: Information Technology, Economic Restructuring, and the Urban-Regional Process*. Oxford: Basil Blackwell.

Cavallo, Guglielmo, and Roger Chartier, eds. 1999. *A History of Reading in the West*. Trans. Lydia G. Cochrane. Amherst: University of Massachusetts Press.

Cento Bull, Anna. 1999. "Regionalism in Italy." In Wagstaff, *Regionalism in the European Union*, 140–57.

———. 2000. *Social Identities and Political Cultures in Italy: Catholic, Communist and 'Leghist' Communities between Civicness and Localism*. New York: Berghahn Books.

Cherland, Meredith Rogers. 1994. *Private Practices: Girls Reading Fiction and Constructing Identity*. London: Taylor & Francis.

Cipolla, Carlo M. 1969. *Literacy and Development in the West*. Baltimore: Penguin Books.

Cole, Susan Guettel. 2004. *Landscapes, Gender, and Ritual Space: The Ancient Greek Experience*. Berkeley: University of California Press.

Coleman, Joyce. 1996. *Public Reading and the Reading Public in Late Medieval England and France*. New York: Cambridge University Press.

Coser, Lewis A. 1965. *Men of Ideas: A Sociologist's View.* New York: Free Press.

Currie, Dawn H. 1999. *Girl Talk: Adolescent Magazines and Their Readers.* Toronto: University of Toronto Press.

Cushman, Grant, A. J. Veal, and Jiri Zuzanek. 1996. *World Leisure Participation Free Time in the Global Village.* Wallingford, Oxon, U.K.: CAP International.

Dainotto, Roberto Maria. 2000. *Place in Literature: Regions, Cultures, Communities.* Ithaca: Cornell University Press.

Darnton, Robert. 1990. *The Kiss of Lamourette: Reflections in Cultural History.* New York: W. W. Norton.

Dennis, James M. 1998. *Renegade Regionalists: The Modern Independence of Grant Wood, Thomas Hart Benton, and John Steuart Curry.* Madison: University of Wisconsin Press.

DiMaggio, Paul. 1997. "Culture and Cognition." *Annual Review of Sociology* 23:263–87.

DiMaggio, Paul, and Francie Ostrower. 1992. *Race, Ethnicity, and Participation in the Arts: Patterns of Participation by Hispanics, Whites, and African-Americans in Selected Activities from the 1982 and 1985 Surveys of Public Participation in the Arts.* Research Division Report no. 25, National Endowment for the Arts. Washington, DC: Seven Locks Press.

Dionisotti, Carlo. 1967. *Geografia e storia della letteratura italiana.* Torino: Giulio Einaudi.

Duneier, Mitchell. 1999. *Sidewalk.* New York: Farrar, Straus and Giroux.

Ehrlich, Eugene, and Gorton Carruth. 1982. *The Oxford Illustrated Guide to the United States.* New York: Oxford University Press.

Eisenstein, Elizabeth L. 1979. *The Printing Press as an Agent of Change: Communications and Cultural Transformations in Early-Modern Europe.* Cambridge: Cambridge University Press.

Ellis, Diane C., and John C. Beresford. 1994. *Trends in Artist Occupations: 1970–1990.* Research Division Report no. 29, National Endowment for the Arts. Washington, DC: Seven Locks Press.

Empson, William. [1935] 1974. *Some Versions of Pastoral.* New York: New Directions.

Erickson, Bonnie H. 1996. "Culture, Class, and Connections." *American Journal of Sociology* 102:217–51.

Ettin, Andrew V. 1984. *Literature and the Pastoral*. New Haven: Yale University Press.

Falk, William W. 2004. *Rooted in Place: Family and Belonging in a Southern Black Community*. New Brunswick: Rutgers University Press.

Farr, Cecilia Konchar. 2005. *Reading Oprah: How Oprah's Book Club Changed the Way America Reads*. Albany: State University of New York Press.

Ferguson, Priscilla Parkhurst. 1987. *Literary France: The Making of a Culture*. Berkeley: University of California Press.

Fernandez, Ramona. 2001. *Imagining Literacy: Rhizomes of Knowledge in American Culture and Literature*. Austin: University of Texas Press.

Finkelstein, Monte S. 1998. *Separatism, the Allies, and the Mafia: The Struggle for Sicilian Independence, 1943–1948*. Bethlehem, PA: Lehigh University Press.

Fischer, David Hackett. 1989. *Albion's Seed: Four British Folkways in America*. New York: Oxford University Press.

Florida, Richard. 2002. Reprinted with a new preface, 2004. *The Rise of the Creative Class: And How It's Transforming Work, Leisure, Community, and Everyday Life*. New York: Basic Books.

Forgacs, David. 1990a. *Italian Culture in the Industrial Era 1880–1980: Cultural Industries, Politics, and the Public*. Manchester: Manchester University Press.

———. 1990b. "The Italian Communist Party and Culture." Ch. 5 in Barański and Lumley 1990, 97–114.

Friedland, Roger, and Deirdre Boden. 1994. *NowHere: Space, Time and Modernity*. Berkeley: University of California Press.

Furet, François, and Jacques Ozouf. 1982. *Reading and Writing: Literacy in France from Calvin to Jules Ferry*. Cambridge: Cambridge University Press.

Gallup Poll. 1990. December Wave 2. Field date 12/13/1990–12/16/1990. Available online at http://institution.gallup.com/documents/questionnaire.aspx?STUDY GNS922024. Accessed Feb. 25, 2005.

———. 1991 February Wave 4. Field date 2/21/1991–2/24/1991. Available online at http://brain.gallup.com/documents/questionnaire.aspx?STUDY=GNS122018.

———. 2001. Gallup Poll Social Series: Lifestyle. Field date: 12/06/2001–12/09/2001. Available online at http://brain.gallup.com/documents/questionnaire.aspx?STUDY=P0112045.

———. 2003a. Social Series: Lifestyle. Field date: 12/11/2003–12/14/2003. Available online at http://brain.gallup.com/documents/questionnaire.aspx?STUDY=P0312053.

———. 2003b. Social Series: Work and Education. Field date 8/4/2003–8/6/2003. Available online at http://brain.gallup.com/documents/questionnaire.aspx?STUDY=P0308039.

Gastil, Raymond D. 1975. *Cultural Regions of the United States*. Seattle: University of Washington Press.

Gautreaux, Tim. 2003. *The Clearing*. New York: Alfred A. Knopf.

General Social Survey. 1998. "Codebook Variable: READFICT." Available online at http://webapp.icpsr.umich.edu/GSS/rnd1998/merged/cdbk/readfict.htm.

Giddens, Anthony. 1990. *The Consequences of Modernity*. Stanford: Stanford University Press.

Gieryn, Thomas F. 2000. "A Space for Place in Sociology." *Annual Review of Sociology 2000*: 463–96.

Gifford, Terry. 1999. *Pastoral*. London: Routledge.

Giglio, Raffaele. 1995. *La letteratura del sole: nuovi studi di letteratura meridionale*. Napoli: Edizioni scientifiche italiane.

Ginsborg, Paul. 1990. *A History of Contemporary Italy: Society and Politics 1943–1988*. London: Penguin.

———. 2003. *Italy and Its Discontents: Family, Civil Society, State: 1980–2001*. New York: Palgrave Macmillan.

Glaeser, Andreas M. 2000. *Divided in Unity: Identity, Germany, and the Berlin Police*. Chicago: University of Chicago Press.

Goody, Jack, ed. 1968. *Literacy in Traditional Societies*. Cambridge: Cambridge University Press.

———. 1977. *The Domestication of the Savage Mind*. Cambridge: Cambridge University Press.

Goody, Jack, and Ian Watt. 1968. "The Consequences of Literacy." In *Literacy in Traditional Societies*, ed. Jack Goody, 27–68. Cambridge: Cambridge University Press. [This article first appeared in *Comparative Studies in Society and History* 5 (April 1963): 304–45.]

Gowan, Barbara, and Katherine Larson. 2002. *G Is for Grand Canyon: An Arizona Alphabet*. Chelsea, MI: Sleeping Bear Press.

Graff, Harvey J. 1987. *The Legacies of Literacy: Continuities and Contradictions in Western Culture and Society.* Bloomington: Indiana University Press.

Griffin, Larry J., and Don H. Doyle, eds. 1995. *The South as an American Problem.* Athens: University of Georgia Press.

Griswold, Wendy. 1993. "Recent Moves in the Sociology of Literature." *Annual Review of Sociology* 19:455–67.

———. 2000. *Bearing Witness: Readers, Writers, and the Novel in Nigeria.* Princeton: Princeton University Press.

———. 2001a. "The Ideas of the Reading Class (in A Symposium on Books)." *Contemporary Sociology* 30, no. 1 (January): 4–6.

———. 2001b. "Regionalism and Cultural Expression." *The International Encyclopedia of the Social and Behavioral Sciences.* Vol. 19:12935–39. Oxford: Elsevier.

Griswold, Wendy, and Fredrik Engelstad. 1998. "Does the Center Imagine the Periphery?: State Support and Literary Regionalism in Norway and the United States." *Comparative Social Research* 17:129–75.

Griswold, Wendy, and Kathleen Hull. 1998. "The Burnished Steel Watch: What a Sample of a Single Year's Fiction Indicates." In *The Empirical Study of Literature and the Media*, ed. Susanne Janssen and Nel van Dijk. Rotterdam, The Netherlands: Barjesteh van Waalwijk van Doorn.

Griswold, Wendy, Terry McDonnell, and Nathan Wright. 2005. "Reading and the Reading Class in the Twenty-First Century." *Annual Review of Sociology* 31:127–41.

Griswold, Wendy, and Nathan Wright. 2004. "Wired and Well Read." In *Society Online: The Internet in Context*, ed. Philip N. Howard and Steve Jones. Thousand Oaks, CA: Sage Publications.

Hagen, Inger Marie. 1996. *Regional Literary Systems in Norway.* Oslo: Institutt for samfunnsforskning.

Hall, Christine, and Martin Coles. 1999. *Children's Reading Choices.* London: Routledge.

Haraway, Donna. 1990. "A Manifesto for Cyborgs." In *Feminism/Postmodernism*, ed. Linda Nicholson. London: Routledge.

Hargittai, Eszter. 2002. "Second-Level Digital Divide: Differences in People's Online Skills." *First Monday: Peer-Reviewed Journal on the Internet* 7, no. 4 (April). http://firstmonday.org/issues/issue7_4/hargittai/index.html.

Harris, William V. 1989. *Ancient Literacy.* Cambridge, MA: Harvard University Press.

Harstad, Donald. 1999. *Known Dead.* New York: Bantam Books.

Hart, James D., ed. 1983. *The Oxford Companion to American Literature.* 5th ed. 1983. New York: Oxford University Press.

Hartley, Jenny. 2001. *Reading Groups. A Survey Conducted in Association with Sara Turvey.* Oxford: Oxford University Press.

Harvey, David. 1990. *The Condition of Postmodernity: An Enquiry into the Origins of Cultural Change.* Cambridge, MA: Blackwell.

———. 1993. "From Space to Place and Back Again: Reflections on the Condition of Postmodernity." In *Mapping the Futures,* Bird et al. 1993, 3–29.

Henmo, S. 1996. *Lesing av regional litteratur.* MA Thesis, Department of Sociology and Human Geography, University of Oslo.

Henrichsen, Bjørn, and Stein Rokkan. 1977. *Kommunedatabanken: En handbook for brukere.* NSD Håndbøker nr. 2. Bergen: Norges Samfunnsvitenskapelige Datatjeneste.

Hirsch, Paul M. 1972. "Processing Fads and Fashions." *American Journal of Sociology* 77:639–59.

Hochschild, Arlie Russell. 1997. *The Time Bind: When Work Becomes Home and Home Becomes Work.* New York: Metropolitan Books.

Huffman, James L. 1997. *Creating a Public: People and Press in Meiji Japan.* Honolulu: University of Hawai'i Press.

ISTAT (Istituto nazionale di statistica). 2005. "Cultura, Socialità et tempo libero, Anno 2003." Famiglia e società: Novità Editoriale. 21 Guigno.

IT & Society. 2002. "IT, Mass Media, and Other Daily Activity," vol. 1, issue 2. John P. Robinson, special editor. Fall 2002.http://www.stanford.edu/group/siqss/itandsociety/v01i02.html.

Iyer, Pico. 2000. *The Global Soul: Jet Lag, Shopping Malls, and the Search for Home.* New York: Knopf.

Jakle, John, and Keith A. Sculle. 1994. *The Gas Station in America.* Baltimore: Johns Hopkins University Press.

———. 1999. *Fast Food: Roadside Restaurants in the Automobile Age.* Baltimore: Johns Hopkins University Press.

———. 2004. *Lots of Parking: Land Use in a Car Culture.* Charlottesville: University of Virginia Press.

Jakle, John, Keith A. Sculle, and Jefferson S. Rogers. 1996. *The Motel in America*. Baltimore: Johns Hopkins University Press.

Jensen, Merrill, ed. 1952/1965. *Regionalism in America*. Repr. Madison: University of Wisconsin Press.

Johansson, Egil. 1977. *The History of Literacy in Sweden: In Comparison with Some Other Countries* (Educational reports Umeå). Sweden: Umeå University and Umeå School of Education.

Jordan, David, ed. 1994. *Regionalism Reconsidered: New Approaches to the Field*. New York: Garland.

Keating, Michael. 1997. "The Invention of Regions: Political Restructuring and Territorial Government in Western Europe." *Environment and Planning C: Government and Policy* 15:383–98.

Kern, Stephen. 1983. *The Culture of Time and Space: 1880–1918*. Cambridge, MA: Harvard University Press.

Kittredge, William, and Annick Smith, eds. 1988. *The Last Best Place: A Montana Anthology*. Seattle: University of Washington Press.

Klinenberg, Eric. 2002. *Heat Wave: A Social Autopsy of Disaster in Chicago*. Chicago: University of Chicago Press.

Knight, Stephen. 1995. "Regional Crime Squads: Location and Dislocation in the British Mystery." Ch. 3 in *Peripheral Visions: Images of Nationhood in Contemporary British Fiction*, ed. Ian A. Bell. Cardiff: University of Wales Press.

Knulst, W., and G. Kraaykamp. 1998. "Trends in leisure reading: Forty years of research on reading in the Netherlands." *Poetics* 26 (1): 21–41.

Knulst, Wim, and Gerbert Kraaykamp. 1997. "The Decline of Reading: Leisure Reading Trends in the Netherlands (1955–1995)." *Netherlands' Journal of Social Sciences* 33:130–50.

Lash, Scott, and John Urry. 1994. *Economies of Signs and Space*. London: Sage Publications.

Lee, Felicia R. 2004. "Chick-Lit King Imagines His Way into Women's Heads." *New York Times*. July 29. http://www.ericjeromedickey.com/media/nytimes.htm.

Lepschy, Giulio. 1990. "How Popular Is Italian?" Ch. 3 in Barański and Lumley 1990, 63–78.

Levine, Lawrence W. 1988. *Highbrow/Lowbrow: The Emergence of Cultural Hierarchy in America*. Cambridge, MA: Harvard University Press.

Levy, Carlo, ed. 1996. *Italian Regionalism: History, Identity and Politics.* Oxford: Berg.

Link, Perry. 1981. *Mandarin Ducks and Butterflies: Popular Fiction in Early Twentieth-Century Chinese Cities.* Berkeley: University of California Press.

Logan, John R., and Harvey L. Molotch. 1988. *Urban Fortunes: Political Economy of Place.* Berkeley: University of California Press.

Long, Elizabeth. 2003. *Book Clubs: Women and the Uses of Reading in Everyday Life.* Chicago: University of Chicago Press.

Lowenthal, David. 1985. *The Past Is a Foreign Country.* Cambridge: Cambridge University Press.

Lumley, Robert. 1996. "Peculiarities of the Italian Newspaper." Ch. 11 in Forgacs and Lumley 1996, 199–215.

MacCannell, Dean. 1976. *The Tourist: A New Theory of the Leisure Class.* New York: Schocken Books.

Mackin, Bob. 2006. "36 Hours in Whitehorse." *New York Times,* January 27.

Maffesoli, Michel. 1988. *Le Temps des tribus.* Paris: Méridiens Klincksieck.

———. 1996. *The Time of the Tribes: The Decline of Individualism in Mass Society.* Trans. Don Smith. London: Sage Publications.

Maine Literature Project, Jeff Fischer, director. 1989. *Maine Speaks: An Anthology of Maine Writers.* Brunswick, ME: Maine Writers & Publishers Alliance.

Manguel, Alberto. 1996. *A History of Reading.* New York: Penguin.

Marx, Karl. 1993. *Grundrisse: Foundations of the Critique of Political Economy (rough draft).* Trans. with a foreword by Martin Nicolaus. London: Penguin Books, in association with New Left Review.

Massey, Doreen. 1984. *Spatial Divisions of Labour: Social Structures and the Geography of Production.* Houndmills: Macmillan.

———. 1993. "Power-Geometry and a Progressive Sense of Place." In Bird et al. 1993, 59–69.

Massey, Douglas S., and Nancy A. Denton. 1994. *American Apartheid: Segregation and the Making of the Underclass.* Cambridge, MA: Harvard University Press.

Maurer, Doris, and Arnold E. Maurer. 1993. *Guida letteraria Dell'Italia.* Milano: TEA—Tascabili degli Editori Associati S.p.A.

Mauri, Paolo. 1989. "La Liguria." In Asor Rosa 1989, 339–84.

Mauri, Stefano. 1987. *Il Libro in Italia: Geografia, Produzione, Consumo.* Milano: Ulrico Hoepli Editore.

Mee, Susan, ed. 1995. *Downhome: An Anthology of Southern Women Writers.* San Diego: Harcourt.

Meinig, D. W. 1986. *Atlantic America, 1492–1800.* Vol. 1 of *The Shaping of America: A Geographical Perspective on 500 Years of History.* New Haven: Yale University Press.

Melucci, Alberto. 1989. *Nomads of the Present: Social Movements and Individual Needs in Contemporary Society.* Ed. John Keane and Paul Mier. London: Century Hutchinson.

Meyrowitz, Joshua. 1985. *No Sense of Place: The Impact of Electronic Media on Social Behavior.* New York: Oxford University Press.

Miller, Laura J. 2006. *Reluctant Capitalists: Bookselling and the Culture of Consumption.* Chicago: University of Chicago Press.

National Endowment for the Arts. 1998. *1997 Survey of Public Participation in the Arts.* Washington, DC: National Endowment for the Arts.

———. 2004a. *Reading At Risk: A Survey of Literary Reading in America.* Research Division Report no. 46. Washington, DC: National Endowment for the Arts.

———. 2004b. *How the United States Funds the Arts.* Washington, DC: National Endowment for the Arts.

Nissenbaum, Stephen. 1996. "New England as Region and Nation." Ch. 2 in Ayers et al. 1996.

Norton Anthology of Literature by Women. 1985. Ed. Sandra M. Gilbert and Susan Gubar. New York: W. W. Norton.

Nowell-Smith, Geoffrey. 1990. "Italy: Tradition, Backwardness and Modernity." Ch. 3 in Barański and Lumley 1990, 50–62.

Odum, Howard Washington, and Harry Estill Moore. 1938. *American Regionalism: A Cultural-Historical Approach to National Integration.* New York: H. Holt.

OECD and Statistics Canada. 1994. *Literacy, Economy and Society: Results of the first International Adult Literacy Survey.* Paris: Organisation for Economic Co-Operation and Development/Statistics Canada.

———. 2000. *Literacy in the Information Age: Final Report of the International Adult Literacy Survey.* Paris: Organisation for Economic Co-operation and Development Publishing/Statistics Canada.

Øidne, Gabriel. 1959. "Litt om motsetninga mellom Auslandet og Vetslandet." *Syn og Segn* 63:97–114.

Oldenburg, Ray. 1989. *The Great Good Place: Cafés, Coffee Shops, Community Centers, Beauty Parlors, General Stores, Bars, Hangouts, and How They Get You Through the Day.* New York: Paragon House.

Parush, Iris. 2004. *Reading Jewish Women: Marginality and Modernization in Nineteenth-Century Eastern European Jewish Society.* Trans. Saadya Sternberg. Waltham, MA: Brandeis University Press.

People's Daily Online. 2004. "Chinese People Read Less, Survey." August 18. http://english.people.com.cn/200408/18/eng20040818 _153593.html

Peterson, Richard A., ed. 1976. *The Production of Culture.* Beverly Hills: Sage Publications.

———. 1978. "The Production of Cultural Change: The Case of Contemporary Country Music." *Social Research* 45:292–314.

Peterson, Richard A., and Roger M. Kern. 1996. "Changing Highbrow Taste: From Snob to Omnivore." *American Sociological Review* 61:900–907.

Pietralunga, Mark F. 1990. "Gina Lagorio." In *Contemporary Women Writers in Italy: A Modern Renaissance,* ed. Santo L. Aricò, 76–88. Amherst: University of Massachusetts Press.

Pollock, Sheldon I. 2000. "Cosmopolitan and Vernacular in History." *Public Culture* 12:591–625.

Population Reference Bureau. 2005. "Human Population: Fundamentals of Growth Patterns of World Urbanization." http://www .prb.org/Content/NavigationMenu/PRB/Educators/Human _Population/Urbanization2/Patterns_of_World_Urbanization1.htm

Putnam, Robert D. 1993. *Making Democracy Work: Civic Traditions in Modern Italy.* Princeton: Princeton University Press.

———. 2000. *Bowling Alone: The Collapse and Revival of American Community.* New York: Simon and Schuster.

Raban, Jonathan. 1996. *Bad Land: An American Romance.* New York: Pantheon Books.

Radway, Janice A. 1991. *Reading the Romance: Women, Patriarchy, and Popular Literature.* Repr. Chapel Hill: University of North Carolina Press.

Reading and Buying Books for Pleasure: 2005 National Survey, Final Report. 2005. Submitted to Canadian Heritage: Industry Development Publishing Policy and Programs. Montreal: Créatic.

Reed, John Shelton. 1986. *The Enduring South: Subcultural Persistence in Mass Society.* Chapel Hill: University of North Carolina Press.

Roberts, Donald F., and Ulla G. Foehr. 2004. *Kids and Media in America.* Cambridge: Cambridge University Press.

Rokkan, Stein. 1970. *Citizens, Elections, Parties.* Oslo: Norwegian University Press.

Rose, Jonathan. 2001. *The Intellectual Life of the British Working Classes.* New Haven: Yale University Press.

Ross, Catherine Sheldrick, Lynne E. F. McKechnie, and Paulette M. Rothbauer. 2006. *Reading Matters: What the Research Reveals About Reading, Libraries, and Community.* Westport, CT: Libraries Unlimited.

Ryden, Kent C. 1993. *Mapping the Invisible Landscape.* Iowa City: University of Iowa Press.

Sassen, Saskia. 2001. *The Global City: New York, London, Tokyo.* 2nd ed. Princeton: Princeton University Press.

Sciascia, Leonardo. 1961/2003. *The Day of the Owl* (*Il Giorno della Civetta*). Trans. Archibald Colquhoun and Arthur Oliver; intro. by George Scialabba. Repr. New York: New York Review of Books.

Simpson, Claude M., ed. 1960. *The Local Colorists: American Short Stories, 1857–1900.* New York: Harper and Row.

Smith, Anthony D. 1986. *The Ethnic Origins of Nations.* Oxford: Basil Blackwell.

Spain, Daphne. 1992. *Gendered Spaces.* Chapel Hill: University of North Caroline Press.

Stack, Carol B. 1996. *Call to Home: African Americans Reclaim the Rural South.* New York: Basic Books.

Statistics Norway. 1993. *Inntekts-og formuesstatistikk (1982, 1984–1990).* NOS C70. Oslo: Statistics Norway.

———. 1996a. *Levekårsundersøkelsen 1995.* NOS C301. Oslo: Statistics Norway.

———. 1996b. *Statistisk årbok 1996.* Oslo: Statistics Norway.

———. 2004. Statistical Yearbook of Norway. Oslo: Statistics Norway. http://www.ssb.no/English/yearbook/.

St. Clair, William. 2004. *The Reading Nation in the Romantic Period.* Cambridge: Cambridge University Press.

Stuckey, J. Elspeth. 1991. *The Violence of Literacy.* Portsmouth, NH: Boynton/Cook (Heinemann Educational).

Stussi, Alfredo, ed. 1979. *Letterature italiana e culture regionali.* Bologna: Nicola Zanichelli.

Suttles, Gerald D. 1972. *The Social Construction of Communities.* Chicago: University of Chicago Press.

Swidler, Ann. 1986. "Culture in Action: Symbols and Strategies." *American Sociological Review* 51:273–86.

Theocritus. 1989. *The Idylls.* Trans. with an introduction and notes by Robert Wells. London: Penguin.

Torpey, John. 2000. *The Invention of the Passport: Surveillance, Citizenship and the State.* Cambridge: Cambridge University Press.

Trigilia, Carlo. 1992. "Italian Industrial Districts: Neither Myth nor Interlude." In *Industrial Districts and Local Economic Regeneration,* ed. F. Pyke and W. Sengenberger, 33–47. Geneva: International Institute for Labour Studies.

Tuan, Yi-Fu. 1975. "Place: An Experiential Perspective." *The Geographical Review* 65:151–65.

Tuska, John, and Vicki Pierkarski, eds. 1983. *Encyclopedia of Frontier and Western Fiction.* New York: McGraw Hill.

UNESCO. 2004a. "Regional Youth and Adult Literacy Rates and Illiterate Population by Gender for 2000–2004." September. UNESCO Institute for Statistics, Literacy and Non-Formal Education Section.

———. 2004b. "Youth (15–24) and Adult (15+) Literacy Rates by Country and by Gender for 2000–2004." September. UNESCO Institute for Statistics, Literacy and Non-Formal Education Section.

U.S. Census Bureau. 1996. *Statistical Abstract of the United States: 1996.* Washington, DC: U.S. Department of Commerce, Economics, and Statistical Administration, Bureau of the Census.

———. 2000. *Statistical Abstract of the United States: 2000.* Washington, DC: U.S. Department of Commerce, Economics, and Statistical Administration, Bureau of the Census.

———. 2005. *Statistical Abstract of the United States: 2004–2005.* Section 1: Population. Washington, DC: U.S. Department of

Commerce, Economics, and Statistical Administration, Bureau of the Census.

Van Gelder, Lawrence. 2004. "Hugh Grant in a Page Turner." In the Arts, Briefly column. *New York Times.* December 14.

Wagemaker, Hans, ed. 1996. *Are Girls Better Readers?: Gender Differences in Reading Literacy in 32 Countries.* Amsterdam: International Association for the Evaluation of Educational Achievement.

Wagner, Daniel A., Richard L. Venezky, and Brian V. Street. 1999. *Literacy: An International Handbook.* Boulder, CO: Westview Press.

Wagner-Pacifici, Robin. 2005. *The Art of Surrender: Decomposing Sovereignty at Conflict's End.* Chicago: University of Chicago Press.

Waller, Philip J. 2006. *Writers, Readers, and Reputations: Literary Life in Britain, 1870–1918.* Oxford: Oxford University Press.

Watt, Ian. 1957/1974. *The Rise of the Novel: Studies in Defoe, Richardson, and Fielding.* Repr. Berkeley: University of California Press.

Wells, Robert. 1989. Introduction and notes to Theocritus, *The Idylls.* London: Penguin.

Williams, Raymond. 1977. *Marxism and Literature.* Oxford: Oxford University Press.

Wilson, Charles Reagan, and William Ferris, eds. 1989. *Encyclopedia of Southern Culture.* Sponsored by the Center for the Study of Southern Culture at the University of Mississippi. Chapel Hill: University of North Carolina Press.

Wilson, Harold F. 1936. *The Hill Country of Northern New England; Its Social and Economic History, 1790–1930.* New York: Columbia University Press.

Witte, James C. 2003. "The Case for Multi-Method Research: Large Sample Design and the Study of Life." In *Society Online: The Internet in Context,* ed. Philip E. N. Howard and Steve Jones. Thousand Oaks, CA: Sage Publications.

Witte, James C., Lisa M. Amoroso, and Philip E. N. Howard. 2000. "Method and Representation in Internet-Based Survey Tools: Mobility, Community, and Cultural Identity in Survey 2000." *Social Science Computer Review* 18:179–95.

Witte, James C., and Philip E. N. Howard. 2002. "The Future of Polling: Relational Inference and the Development of Internet Survey Instruments." In *Navigating Public Opinion,* ed. Fay Cook and Jeffrey Manza. Oxford: Oxford University Press.

Wuthnow, Robert. 2006. "Cognition and Religion." Paul Hanly Furfey Lecture, Association for the Sociology of Religion, Montreal, August.

Zerubavel, Eviatar. 1997. *Social Mindscapes*. Cambridge, MA: Harvard University Press.

Zill, Nicholas, and Marianne Winglee. 1990. *Who Reads Literature: The Future of the United States as a Nation of Readers*. Cabin John, MD: Seven Locks Press.

Zukin, Sharon. 1982. *Loft Living: Culture and Capital in Urban Change*. Baltimore: Johns Hopkins University Press.

———. 1991. *Landscapes of Power: From Detroit to Disney World*. Berkeley: University of California Press.

Index